*With God and Two Ducats*

*Mother Mary of the Blessed Sacrament*
*Foundress and Mother General*
*of the Corpus Christi Carmelites*
*1909–1949*

# With God and Two Ducats

## THE STORY OF THE CORPUS CHRISTI

## CARMELITES

## IN THREE COUNTRIES

# 1908-1958

## BY KATHERINE BURTON

THE CARMELITE PRESS

*Chicago, 1958*

271-B98

*"With God and two ducats
I can do anything."*

ST. TERESA'S WRITINGS

# Preface

THE CARMELITE SISTERS OF CORPUS CHRISTI HAVE BEEN AS-
sociated with the archdiocese of Port of Spain ever since
they came into corporate existence through the inspired
zeal of their venerable Foundress, Mother Mary of the
Blessed Sacrament Ellerker. This year occurs the Golden
Jubilee of their foundation, and, by happy coincidence
this year, also, the Congregation has received final ap-
probation from the Holy See, giving it Pontifical status
among the Church's families of religious.

It is very appropriate, then, that an account of its birth
and growth should be made available to those who have
admired the work of the Sisters not only in the West
Indies and British Guiana but in England and the United

States but are unaware of the Congregation's history. Mrs. Katherine Burton has presented the story in her well-known attractive style.

But for those who are able, as the saying goes, "to read between the lines," *With God and Two Ducats* is more than an historical record. It is a "praise of glory" (Ephesians 1) to the unerring Providence of God, "reaching from end to end mightily and disposing all things sweetly" (Wisdom) Who having cast the seed of a Eucharistic word into the receptive heart of a child, gave it the increase which we now see in the many communities of Corpus Christi Carmelites.

The reading of this book may prove to be the sowing of the seed of the Carmelite vocation in many generous hearts desirous of helping to save society through the Eucharistic reign of Jesus Christ our Lord. We earnestly hope it may.

Finbar
March 29th, 1958          Archbishop of Port of Spain

# *Foreword*

TO THE MAJORITY OF PEOPLE IT IS A SURPRISING THING TO learn that there are active religious as well as contemplative in the Carmelite Order, and that they function in many countries, including the United States.

To see a religious in Carmelite garb working among children or with the sick or aged, to see her waiting at a bus stop or driving a station wagon, is apt to be a surprising sight to those who know that the habit which these religious wear is the habit of Carmel.

"But they can't be *real* Carmelites," they will say.

Over and over the religious themselves give an answer to those who know only one kind of Carmelite religious —the one behind the grille, back of the concealing curtain. "We are not cloistered. We are active Carmelites.

We are a missionary group in the Order," they explain.

There is not a great deal of information in books about the active Carmelites. Perhaps they are too busy to write their own history as members of their Order, too busy with the homes for the aged, the orphan asylums, the schools, the hospitals. Perhaps their works are the best answer regarding these continuously growing groups who have no time to write at length about their historical background. Perhaps the practical results are the best answer to the remark, "But you can't be Carmelites."

As a matter of fact, active Carmelite groups go back many hundreds of years. In 1452 a Carmelite father, John Soreth, while in Cologne, founded there a second and a third group of his order. In those days these portions of the order were closely allied with the fraternities and guilds of the day, working with them in a common apostolate.

During that century several communities of beguines, groups of women banded together to pray and to work for the bodies as well as the souls of those in need, asked to be affiliated with the Carmelite Order, wishing to continue their work under the aegis of an established congregation. By the end of the fifteenth century groups of active Carmelites were in many lands—France, Belgium, Spain, Italy. Perhaps back of all this activity was the example of the great Teresa herself: for all that, she was a contemplative nun; she was a great missionary and a traveler for God, when the times and its needs demanded. In fact, the Spanish members of her order were in the beginning more interested in the active life than were those of other lands.

The truth of course is that the active life was a development of the ancient spirit of Carmel. The contemplative life was and is its foundation; the Marian element is its distinctive mark; its active life is an outgrowth of both. And, despite its activity, the special mission of the Carmelite Order and all its members is to teach the art of prayer.

Basically, the Carmelite spirit is one of contemplation and its apostolic activity is secondary. Prayer comes first, but with it the religious must give to others the fruit of that contemplation and lead them to pray. "As the Lord liveth, in whose sight I stand," so Saint Elijah phrased it, the pre-Christian teacher and prophet who is considered the founder of the Carmelite Order.

As for those groups who, beginning with the beguines, asked to enter Carmel, one of the first was established by Anna Puttemans, who in 1663 founded a congregation in France. A second was established by Sister Magdalene de Pazzi who founded a group of religious in Italy in 1724, which a few years later affiliated with Carmel; their chief work was the education of poor children. In Spain the Third Order Sisters of Charity became Carmelite in 1874. Twenty years before that Sister Maria Teresa of Jesus founded an active Carmelite group in Italy. In 1891 a community was founded in Spain to care for the sick in hospital and home. In Brazil another was devoted to education and the care of orphans.

The active Carmelites have a beata. In 1940 Pius XII beatified Sister Joachim of Barcelona, born in 1783, a devoted wife and mother of nine children, who in 1826 founded the Carmelite Sisters of Charity. When she died of cholera in 1854 her congregation had two hundred members.

To one who does not examine it carefully, there seems at first sight a contradiction in the two aims of the contemplative life, the active life. The first is a love of solitude. But in every Carmel which carries on the apostolic work there is among its members this spirit of solitude—and it comes first of all. Each cell is a little desert protected by the Rule from the entrance of anyone, and the solitude is filled with love of God and also with love of silence. The active Carmelites have a part in the contemplative life, too, through their daily life in the Order: like the others, they chant the Divine Office daily in choir and they use for their own the entire ceremonial which the Carmelite Order enjoys.

One good argument for the great need of this portion of the Order is Saint Therese of Lisieux, herself vowed to the contemplative life of Carmel, yet Patroness of Missionaries by decision of the Holy See, and so patroness of an active apostolate.

Thomas Aquinas once said that a very excellent life in religion is one where "contemplation overflows in activity, an activity which is the life of charity."

It is a life like that, contemplation linked with activity, prayer linked with socal service, which has produced such a congregation as that whose story follows—the Corpus Christi Carmelites.

# ONE

$B$ISHOP BRINDLE OF NOTTINGHAM STOOD LOOKING AT THE group of little girls listening intently to a young woman who was telling them a story. He put up his hand for silence to her mother who had met him at the door, heard his errand and was about to bring him forward. Instead, he stood listening to the young woman's words.

"Just one short story about Thérèse Martin when she was a very little girl, and then I must send you home or your mothers will begin to worry," Miss Ellerker was saying. "This is an especially nice one. You see in some churches in France there is a lovely custom of blessing small pieces of bread so that people can take it home to someone who couldn't come to Mass. Because Thérèse was only five years old, she was considered too young to go and so her older sister Celine usually brought home to her a piece of this blessed bread. Thérèse always waited eagerly for her return and when one day her sister came home with nothing for her, the little girl felt very badly. To her this was her share in the Mass.

" 'Then make some,' she said imperiously to Celine, and the latter went to the cupboard and cut a tiny piece from a loaf of bread. She said a Hail Mary over it very solemnly and then handed it to her little sister who ate it with equal solemnity. 'It tastes exactly like the real blessed bread,' she told Celine happily. And some day when you girls are a little older you can read this story yourselves and many more about Thérèse in her convent in Lisieux and about her short and wonderful life."

It was the glance of the children which showed her that someone had come in. When she turned around she was somewhat flustered to realize that it was the Bishop of Nottingham and that he had very obviously been listening to her story telling.

"My Lord, I didn't know you were here," she said, dropping to her knees to kiss his ring.

He smiled. "I wanted to hear the end of the story," he told her, "and I wouldn't let your mother announce me until it was finished."

"I was telling them about Thérèse today because this is the feast day of Our Lady of Mount Carmel," she explained to him. The children had risen and were waiting to go. The Bishop blessed them all and told them to run away until the next story hour. "I wish I could come here too to listen to the next one," he said.

When they had gone, he told Miss Ellerker why he had come: it was to ask if she would open for him a school for Catholic children in the city of Leicester which was in his diocese. The need was great, for Catholic children were receiving little if any religious education. The Bishop knew of her fine reputation as a teacher and that she had for some years been teaching in academies. What he planned was of course somewhat different: a secondary school for girls where a small fee would be asked. He added sadly that he could not offer her much money to open it; he was himself poor.

He had another idea which he thought could perhaps be incorporated later. After the school was well started, perhaps she could carry out certain social works—catechetical teaching, retreats, work with converts—all of which were badly needed and lacking for Leicester. He knew she had had experience in London with such work.

She hesitated. "It is exactly the kind of thing I should like most of all to do," she said. "But if I accepted your offer, I should have to make some arrangement about my present work. Please give me a little time to decide—at least until the end of the school term." He was very willing to wait, he told her, and said goodbye.

After he had gone, she said to her mother, "I wanted to say yes to him right away but I'm afraid I couldn't do well enough all he wants me to. The teaching would be easy enough. I've had plenty of experience. And I do know something about social service work. But to take a house in charge—I never ran a house in my life, mother!"

"If you decide to accept his offer," said Mrs. Perrins, looking at her daughter thoughtfully, "perhaps I'll come with you. You will need someone to look out for your body while you are looking after souls."

Queenie Ellerker gave long thought to the matter, but

there was little doubt in her mind or her mother's—or, in fact, in the Bishop's for he knew her well—that she would accept. Years later, when the work at Leicester had more than justified the Bishop's hopes, Father Vincent McNabb, the Dominican who was to be one of the most important forces in her years at Leicester, said, "I never once asked her to undertake anything for souls and met with a refusal." It was to be the pattern of her life and her work.

Not long after the Bishop's visit, she wrote to tell him that she had decided to accept his offer. By the next year, 1908, she would be ready to begin. "I shall do whatever you find for me to do," she wrote.

Not only the Bishop was delighted but so was Archbishop Illsley of St. Chad's Cathedral in Birmingham. He wrote that he was especially happy to learn that the basic intention of the new work was to be the reunion of Christendom. Delighted also was Queenie Ellerker's friend Mother Mechtilde Thelan of the Sisters of Charity of St. Paul the Apostle in that city and others who knew well the young woman's capabilities and her fervor.

When she was born, on January 12, 1876, she had been baptized in the Protestant church at Handsworth, the suburb of Birmingham, England, where the Perrins family lived. She was given the names of Clara Rose Martha. Though as a child she was called by the name of Clara, in later years she was known among her friends as Queenie.

Her family and their friends were intensely Protestant in convictions, interested in the extensive mission work of their church, and devoted to their Protestant beliefs. There was little doubt that Queenie Ellerker's later interest in social work began in the circle of her own family and their deep interest in that field.

There was also, in the years during which she was growing up, great and often bitter controversy in matters of religion. One portion of the Anglican church had become very Catholic, very devoted to what they called a return to the old Faith and what the more Protestant minded called popery. There had been, and were still to be, long years of arguments on these subjects. They had been going on ever since Dr. John Newman, Oxford scholar and beloved clergyman of the Established Church, had left it for the Catholic Church. Many had followed him, while other good and learned men, like Pusey and Keble, had remained within the framework of the Church of England. The movement had grown stronger with the years; it had become in part a struggle of churchmen who resisted secular authority in spiritual affairs. At the same time it had a much deeper reason: the desire to bring back again to England her church of former centuries, when that country had been known as Our Lady's Dower.

Clara Perrins was too young to understand or care about the discussions and debates of either side of the controversy, but one day when she was still very small she overheard a conversation between her father and a friend of his. Something which the latter said caught the child's attention.

"My sister and I were brought up as good Protestants," said the visitor thoughtfully, "and we learned the Bible well. I don't believe nowadays in what it says but I do think that these Catholics and people like Newman are in a way sensible. They take what the Bible says literally."

Mr. Perrins merely shrugged his shoulders without saying anything, but his visitor went on speaking. It was his very serious tone that made the little girl listen. "I do remember my Bible still and there is one statement I never forgot. 'This is My Body,' it says."

The child caught this phrase and also what the visitor said next. "And that is what Catholics believe you know —that God is really there in everyone of their churches." The two men left the room and she heard nothing more. But the words stayed in her mind—"This is My Body"— and so did the idea of a church with God in it all the time. Then and there she made up her mind that some day she would belong to that church—the one with God in it. Young as she was, she kept that wonderful phrase in the back of her mind.

She was nine years old when she decided to give her mother a fine present for her birthday—an illustrated Bible. She wanted to earn the money to pay for it for herself or it would not be a real present. If her father gave her the money it would be his gift and not her own.

With the help of the cook she filled small bottles with a peppermint solution and these she sold at the houses of neighbors at a penny a little bottle, always carefully explaining the purpose for which she was selling them. Despite the fact that they sold for only a penny and that it took a long time to get the money together, she managed to sell enough to present the Bible to her astonished and delighted mother on her birthday.

One day, remembering the phrase of her father's visitor a few years before, she looked into the Bible to see if she could find it. She was old enough now to know she must look in the New Testament, but even so it took a long search before she found it.

She saw the very words before her eyes: "This is My Body," just as her father's friend had said. As she sat reading them over and over, she heard the bell ring for dinner. Hurrying to the dining-room, she announced to her astonished family, "I'm going to be a Catholic some day when I get big."

Her amazed parents looked at her and then at each other. In that glance was understanding and obvious agreement on how to handle their daughter's outburst. Neither of them spoke angrily to her nor did they argue or laugh. After a moment Mr. Perrins began to talk to his wife on a totally different topic.

Clara Perrins did not make another such statement to her family for some years. She was fourteen years old when she announced that now she was ready to become a Catholic. By that time her father had no doubt forgotten what she had once said or, if he ever thought of it, he decided she too had forgotten about it. However, when she spoke of it this time, he realized that she was no longer a child and her remarks could not be merely ignored.

What he did not know was that in the intervening years she had learned something about the Catholic Church. She had ventured into the Catholic cathedral in Birmingham and looked at all of it—the statues, the flickering lights in red and blue glasses, the wide altar, the little chapels,—the place where God was all the time. Again she had repeated to herself the wonderful words —"This is My Body"—and told herself that some day she would belong to the church which had God in it all the time. During the past year, knowing there might be opposition to her hopes, for she knew her father was a devout Protestant who could not be expected to understand her point of view, she had gone to a friend of the family who was a Catholic. Mrs. Price, who was of a family as cultured and educated as her own, listened with sympathy to the young girl and promised to find out if there was a way in which a young girl who was a minor in the eyes of the law could legally become a Catholic without the consent of her legal guardian, in this case her father.

The lawyer whom Mrs. Price consulted said that the English law was strict in this matter and Clara would have to have her father's consent before taking such a step. When she was of age she could of course do as she pleased. He added that the law applied only to girls who lived at home and were dependent on their parents for support. To become a Catholic now she would, if her father did not approve of the step, have to leave home and earn her own living. All this her friend told her and added, "There would of course be only one kind of work open to you and that would be domestic labor—that is, to live out in service."

The young girl looked troubled, evidently not thinking so much of her own difficulties as the fact that she might hurt her family. Then her face cleared. "Mrs. Price, I'd be willing to work in that way if I had to, even away from home," she said with conviction in her voice, "anything at all if I could be a Catholic."

When, no doubt inwardly afraid but outwardly quiet, Clara told her father all this, he said little at first. To have his daughter become a Catholic was certainly far from his intentions for her future. He knew he had one weapon: if she did leave home, as she had said she would do if he refused his permission, he could go to court and have her ordered to return since she was a minor and he was able and willing to support her. Both parents knew it would create an impossible situation in a family of their position to have a daughter go out in service. He appealed once more to Clara to give up her intention and found her immovable. In a way he admired her determination, for he knew she had inherited that quality from him.

In the end he offered no great opposition to her intention. Instead, he suggested he send her to the Catholic academy of her choice. To this she agreed and spent the next two years at the academy of the Sisters of the Assumption in London. Her decision to become a Catholic grew steadily stronger. Not long after her sixteenth birthday she was received into the Church by Father Pope of the Birmingham Oratory Fathers.

A few years after she entered the Church, Clara Perrins had her surname legally changed to that of a Catholic ancestor of long ago on her mother's side of the family. From that time, and on all papers and in future legal matters, her name was Clara Ellerker. Among her friends, however, she was usually known by the affectionate nickname of Queenie.

The name Ellerker was one quite common in Yorkshire; it cropped up fairly often in historical accounts of early centuries in England. Its best known member was Ralph Ellerker who had fought in the army of Henry VIII and had been with him in France. In 1533, he took part in the great battle of Flodden Field when the English forces defeated the invading Scottish armies. The

King knighted Ralph Ellerker on the field of battle.

In later years he broke with the King for he was a staunch Catholic and could not brook the looting of monasteries and convents. In fact, Sir Ralph was a part of the great Pilgrimage of Grace, the protest in 1536 against the break with the papacy two years before and the confiscation of church properties in the following year. In Yorkshire was held a great rally which gathered strength in numbers from day to day. A huge banner had been made by Catholic ladies for the pilgrims to carry at their head. It depicted the five wounds of Christ, a devotion very popular at the time. The honor of carrying the banner was given to Sir Ralph Ellerker.

The great cavalcade had in it men from all walks of life, among them the Duke of Norfolk and the Duke of Shrewsbury and many of humbler rank. Some of the groups actually managed to secure the return and the reopening of several monasteries and the return of the monks who had been driven from them. Later, on a promise of future action by Parliament on these matters, and of a pardon from the King for those who had taken part in the pilgrimage, the men dispersed and went to their homes.

The promise was not kept; many received death instead of pardon from their king. In later years the Ellerker properties were lost to the crown and some of the family had drifted from the Faith, though others remained loyal.

The girl of that family who had become a Catholic had adopted the name of her long ago ancestor as her own. He had fought in defense of that Faith. Now his descendant was a part of it too.

## *T W O*

Q<small>UEENIE</small> E<small>LLERKER</small> <small>ACQUIRED COLLEGE DEGREES AS THE</small> years passed, among them Licentiate of Arts at St. Andrew's University in Edinburgh, the highest honor a woman could at the time receive in United Kingdom university circles. She had taught in various schools to earn the money for further study. For some years she had taught with the Assumptionist Sisters in the academy where later her younger sister Ethel was to be a pupil, and at Olton Court in Birmingham, where she was teaching at the time the Bishop of Nottingham came to enlist her help in his project.

Over the years some of her family too had been drawn closer to the Church. They were grown up now and had gone their own ways. Mr. Perrins had died a few years before; only Mabel and young Ethel were still at home with their mother.

It was Ethel who was the direct result that other of the family became Catholics. She had been interested in her sister Clara's brave step of some years before and one day asked her mother if she might learn something about the Catholic Church. Mrs. Perrins agreed and realized a priest could best give her such information. She decided, however to go with her daughter so that, if arguments were put forward of which she could not approve, she could object. The result of this venture was that after the question period it turned into an instruction period. Both Mrs. Perrins and Ethel entered the Church, received by Father John Gibbons of Birmingham. Evidently he had answered Ethel's questions very well. In the following year the third daughter, Mabel also entered the Church. It was now a completely Catholic household.

When Ethel was fifteen, she was very anxious to enter the cloistered Carmelites. Queenie, who had herself a deep affection for the traditions of that Order, and especially for young Thérèse Martin, was sorry to learn that, after a brief trial, Ethel could not be accepted because her delicate health forbade the austerities of that life. The disappointment to her little sister was deep, and the older prayed that, even if the physical reality of Carmel could not be granted to Ethel, the many spiritual values would be hers to hold always.

In July, 1908, on the feast of Our Lady of Mount Carmel, Queenie Ellerker started the new work in Leicester. With her, as she had said she would, went her mother, and also the youngest daughter Ethel. The house they were to occupy had been rented the month before.

The three left for Leicester, filled with the solemn feelings of beginning a new life, and one which was to have religion as its base, even though they would be working as laity. They had come with one intention: to work for God's church and God's children, in any way they might be asked.

As often happens when such a high aim is undertaken, the solemnity of their arrival, which had seemed to them rather like a pilgrimage to a shrine, was rudely turned into something very different. Waiting for them on their door step was a small boy, sent there as a boarder under the delusion that a school had already opened.

They comforted the forlorn child and assured him he could stay. There were as yet no beds; the van which was to bring them had not yet come. For themselves they did not mind but they felt the child must have some kind of bed. They took the wrappings from furniture which had arrived and, after giving him a meal from food they had brought with them, they put him on the pile of wrappings and he went quietly to sleep. As for themselves they lay down on the floor in their coats.

By five in the morning they were up though their boarder was still sleeping soundly in his warm cocoon of wrappings. Ethel decided that first of all she would wash the outside steps of the house for they were extremely dirty. "I'll always get up early and do it," she promised, "because the neighbors might think it odd if they saw me doing it later."

Then the three made a brief meditation, for they had decided to invest this new life with some religious activity. They had of course no sort of oratory. The first meditation in the new house was made in what would later be the refectory, and in the dark. They had a few candles but no candlesticks, and so they held the lighted candle by turns, sitting in their wraps on the floor.

A little before seven they lighted the gas, turned the flame low, put on water to heat, and went to the near-by Dominican church for Mass.

After the first day things were easier. Beds came and so did candlesticks. Food was bought and Mrs. Perrins took on herself the cooking of the meals, not too heavy a task for the menus were to be very simple. Their first supper was bread, cheese, cocoa made with water; later meals were equally plain. Desserts, they had decided, they would have only on Sundays and on great feasts.

The house which they had rented in Upper New Walk was not in very good condition when they came there. The three did all the cleaning of it as well as the painting which it needed badly. When their labors were completed, it was a pleasant home and they were able to relax a little. During the evenings of their first weeks in Leicester, after the day's work was over, they read aloud to each other—a life of Saint Dominic, the autobiography of Thérèse Martin, parts of the Divine Office.

Even in their first week in Leicester they had one visitor who came several times to see them, and who was to become their close friend and helper and later their spiritual director—Father Vincent McNabb, prior of the Dominican priory not far from their own house. He had taken an immediate interest in the new group, for he had heard from the Dominican Father Wilberforce a great deal about Miss Ellerker whom he had known well in London.

From the first they talked freely about their plans for the future and also about their immediate problems of the present. One evening they were talking together about their present precarious situation, for that was what it had become. It was not only a matter of money but a place to live. Not long after they had painted and papered their new home and cleaned it thoroughly, they found they would have to leave it. The rains came in floods into the rooms through a bad leak in the roof. The rooms were all but inundated and the people who lived in them had to take shelter in a Dominican convent in the city until they found a new home, this time in the West Walk.

Once when Father McNabb was with them and they were talking about their difficulties, he shook his head reproachfully at such misgivings. "Look, my dear children," he said, "in a way your situation is like that of Our Lord. He never knows where He will be lodged—in some slum or perhaps on the lips of a sacrilegious communicant or in a palace or in the heart of a saint. To have no lasting home is a glorious privilege you share with Him."

On December 8, 1908, Father McNabb recorded the reception in the Leicester Tertiary Chapter of a new member: "Received the habit at my hands, Clara Ellerker, taking the name of Mary of the Blessed Sacrament. Fr. Vincent, Prior." A year later he added another line: "Professed a year later on the same date."

On the day in 1908 when Queenie Ellerker was received, three other names were noted as tertiaries received that day: Anne McDiarmid, a friend of Father McNabb, Mrs. Perrins and Lucy Fowler, a deaf girl who had come to help the newcomers with the housework.

There had been some disappointment at first about the people whom Bishop Brindle had been confident would come to join them. Either they did not appear, after offering to come, or, if they came, they soon went away again, finding the life too hard, the inconveniences too great, the group too small and informal. It would have been little wonder if the pioneer band of three had also decided there was no future in the work they had undertaken, for a permanent home or more religious workers began to seem like a dream for which there would be no reality.

But there were important people who encouraged them. Bishop Brindle refused to be discouraged and sent them needed funds. Archbishop Illsley of Birmingham helped with both money and advice, as did Bishop Keating of Northampton. And they were never to forget the motherly kindness of the Sisters of St. Paul the Apostle.

But it was Father McNabb who gave the most of all. He took them under his white Dominican wing from the very beginning. The analogy was a good one, for he sheltered them in every way. He met every difficulty with spiritual help or managed to produce some material aid.

"To be poor and unpopular is a sure way to Father Vincent's heart," said one priest to Miss Ellerker, and she knew that was certainly true in their case. For conservative England did not take kindly to new religious groups and especially to one like this small one which was literally founding itself and reaching towards forms of social work considered very novel at the time. But Father McNabb was a genius who could produce from his store of friends the very ones who saw eye to eye with them and who would encourage them to persevere.

*Very Reverend Vincent McNabb, O.P.*

It was Father McNabb who brought them two women who were to mean a great deal to them during the next years. The first was Anne McDiarmid, from London, who came several times to visit before she decided to throw in her lot with them. She was the possessor of a master's degree from the university. She was not a young woman; she was in fact almost fifty years old but there was a wonderful spirit of youth about her. The first time she came to see them she brought with her Newman's *Dream of Gerontius* and read it aloud with such love and devotion in her voice that it seemed to those who heard her that everyone must share her own glowing faith.

She and Queenie Ellerker had known each other slightly in London, as had another newcomer to the house in Leicester—Emily Fortey, also one of Father Mc-Nabb's converts. She had been received into the Church in 1884, when she was eighteen, with her father's permission and with the blessing of Cardinal Newman to whom she had written for advice about the step. Emily had a university education but she preferred to live among the poor and unlearned. She was more of a Franciscan than a Dominican, said her friends. As the years went by she developed for herself a semi-habit, a claret colored dress and veil and a black cloak. For a time she had tried the Benedictine vocation but decided her vocation was to be in the world even if not of it. Father Vincent had suggested she join the group at Leicester and she felt very much at home there.

"I like your ideas," she said in her decided way, when they had explained what they hoped to do in the future in addition to their school. "The Church to me is not a haven so much as a field of spiritual activity. I'd never want to be a parasite on the religious life," she added passionately.

Like Anne McDiarmid, her coming was to bring the little group a measure of independence; she was a woman of means who spent freely. "She is like the people of the days of faith who used to give up their goods of this world and make themselves poor for Christ's sake," said Miss Ellerker of their new friend who, she soon found out, gave away everything and bought nothing for herself. Even her shoes were always all but worn out. An old cloak given her by a friend—"just until you get a new one"—she was still wearing years later.

It was no doubt an oddly assorted little group who lived together in the house at Leicester. But they had fine qualities in common—good intellects, a sound faith, a love of God's people, a willingness to serve them, and they shared a sense of joy in this vocation of theirs. It was a very small beginning in the way of a foundation, but it was to develop into what Father McNabb was later to call "an epic of apostolicity."

# *THREE*

T HEY HAD MOVED INTO THEIR HOUSE IN THE WEST WALK
early in January, on the feast of Saint Hilary. "His name
is a good omen," said Ethel. "It means joy and we want
to be a house of joy."

Five made up the group now—Mrs. Perrins and her
two daughters, Emily Fortey, and Lucy Fowler. Lucy was
a very valuable member; because she took over so much
of the housework, it gave the others a chance to do better
the work to which the Bishop had called them. But they
could all cook if the need arose. Emily Fortey was especially noted for her praiseworthy scones; as for clean steps,
no one could make them as snowy as could Ethel.

The new house had a name—The Limes—but the
group now living there had no intention of keeping it.

They wanted a name which would show they were a house of faith. They discussed the matter for some time, and eventually Father McNabb came up with a name which they thought perfect: Corpus Christi House. And so it was named.

One day Emily Fortey, who had been looking at interesting landmarks of the ancient town, learned that the most important guild in Leicester in earlier centuries had been the Corpus Christi Guild. It had been a great center for Catholic works, with especial attention to the care of the sick and Christian education for the young. In the old guild hall she found a window on which some of the glass still showed a modification of the guild badge of centuries ago, a depiction of the Five Wounds, the great popular devotion of those days.

When she came home with this information she was surprised at the response of Miss Ellerker. "Oh, Emily, an ancestor of mine was the man who carried the banner embroidered with that emblem in the Pilgrimage of Grace. Oh, I wish we could have it made and put over our door."

It was Miss Charteris, an artist living in Leicester, and with whom they had become acquainted, who made for them a copy of the badge. They placed it above the door of Corpus Christi House and to it added the motto: "Ego Sum Panis Vitae."

Later Queenie Ellerker had designed a medal, on it the Cup and the Host, as it had been on the banner which Ralph Ellerker carried on the pilgrimage, as it had been on the ancient design of the Leicester Corpus Christi Guild and which was now placed over the door of their house which bore that name.

The group at Corpus Christi House had read further about the history of this title and so learned the beginnings of the feast of Corpus Christi and its cult, which went as far back as the eleventh century. Before that no one had ever denied the Real Presence on the altar. In that century an archbishop of Angers did deny it. He was refuted and a council was held in which the doctrine of Transubstantiation was clearly defined. The archbishop eventually, after having done the harm, submitted to the definition with the rest of the Church.

However, it was Blessed Juliana of Cornillon, brought up by the Franciscan sisters at Liége and allowed to enter their congregation when she was only fourteen, to whom came the idea of making it a feast. She was still very young when she heard a Voice urging her to speak of the adoption of a feast honoring the Sacrament of the altar. For twenty years, feeling herself too humble to bring forward such a suggestion, she kept it secret. Eventually, when she had become prioress of her convent, she confided to a very holy priest what she had been told to do and he consulted with others about it. In 1246 the Bishop of Liége ordered a feast of Corpus Christi celebrated in his diocese. Twenty years later Pope Urban IV extended it to be observed universally. With the centuries it became one of the most touching and lovely of feasts.

It had been a distressing thing to the newcomers to Leicester to find that little interest was being taken in the new Catholic school to be opened there. This was perhaps due to the fact that two previous attempts had ended in failure. However, they went ahead with preparations and planned to open their school in February of 1909, cheered on by the optimistic hopes of Father McNabb.

On January 31 he preached the first sermon in their little chapel. Present were the four who had been first to come and several visitors: Anne McDiarmid, who was still making up her mind about joining them, and two women, aunt and niece, Katherine Bradley and Edith Cooper, who wrote poetry together under the joint pen name of Michael Field. All were converts of Father Mc-Nabb and all were Dominican tertiaries.

He spoke as carefully to the few before him as if it were one of his large audiences. It was clear how much hope he was placing in this little group. "There is a sense in which things are always at a crisis," he began. "The world is always at a crisis and under the need of a great redemption. For the Christian Redemption is not some finished thing, some past episode in history; it is something going on all the time. The death of Christ is not the final act in the redemption of the world. It is a continuing drama of which the opening act is the prologue spoken from the Cross."

It would be their duty, he said, "in this fair land of your birth which is not altogether holy or beautiful, to help awaken the people to a realization of the need of a great redemption." That the women before him had listened to the words, "Come over to Macedonia and help us," he praised highly. "Many think perhaps that you are foolish," he told them. "They are not aware of any crisis and so they look on the step you took as unaccountable." Then he warned his listeners of one thing: "It would be wrong to begin your work here with the thought of your own usefulness. We shall indeed have something to give, but it will not be our own; it will be Christ's."

He spoke of the great Eucharistic congress just ended in London—"and now we are here dedicating our own little Bethlehem to the Body of Christ." They would no doubt meet with trials—"but beginnings would be almost wrong if they were not stamped with the Cross. It is a guarantee, a warrant." Each would meet with her special difficulties—"but the Bread of Life will keep each one's hope alive, her resolution alive, her courage alive."

He knew that they had met with one disappointment—that their coming to open a school had met with some indifference. But already they were planning additional works, such as social settlement projects. It was why, almost from the beginning, they recited the Divine Office in common and adopted certain monastic observances. Their work was to be done always against a background of prayer.

Already Father McNabb was sending people to them, women who needed to talk out their troubles or who were under grave mental strain or were overworked. Many of them were interested in the Church and were half ready to enter; these Queenie and Emily instructed. In fact, at that time began the writing of the books which were to come from the Ellerker pen, then and in later years. She would write a chapter, read it to those who came to see her, make suggested changes. Later these chapters became the books—called Corpus Christi Books—a *Wreath of Feasts, God's Wonder Book, Master, Where Dwellest Thou?,* and many more—all published by Burns, Oates in London.

The group at Corpus Christi went ahead with their preparations for a school, and early in February it was ready to open. Bishop Brindle had promised to come for the dedication and open it formally. Some sixty people were invited, the list made out by the fathers at the priory, for the newcomers as yet knew few people in Leicester.

Father McNabb gave a welcoming address and the Bishop gave a short talk. Miss Fortey thanked him for coming and spoke of the Catholic Women's League which was soon to be established in Leicester. Tea was served.

Nearly everyone who had been invited came. It was a pleasant party. Father Gibbons, who had received Mrs. Perrins, together with Ethel and Mabel, into the Church, came and stayed for the night, next morning saying Mass for the Corpus Christi members at the Mary Chapel in Holy Cross Church.

The Bishop stayed a while after the guests went home, to talk of the new work and of the school. He assured them he knew they would succeed and told them they could count always on his help and his backing. He was a man of great simplicity. As they sat together in the pleasant little parlor talking of the future, the fire began to fail and he went down on one knee at the fireplace, folded a sheet of newspaper, and coaxed the little blaze along until it burned up brightly again.

In March a novena was begun at Corpus Christi House for a very special intention: that Anne McDiarmid would surely come to join them permanently, as she had half promised she would. One evening, while the novena was going on, several members had been away from the house at the time it was usually said, and so it was forgotten. Close to midnight, when everyone was asleep, Ethel wakened and suddenly remembered that no novena prayers had been said that evening.

The others were wakened by a knocking at their doors and Ethel's voice pleading with them to get up so that the novena would not be broken. A compromise was agreed on: Ethel sat on the landing with the book and a candle and the prayers were said with all doors open. Not long after the novena ended, on the feast of the Annunciation, the longed-for new member arrived, ready for work. For all her fifty years, she was a vivacious beautiful woman with warm color in her cheeks and sparkling eyes, very active and able to inspire others.

On the feast of Saint Catherine of Alexandria another novena was begun, this time with the intention of securing badly-needed funds for the school; the response in number of pupils had been larger than they had expected and initial expenses were heavy. To this novena they received an answer too, but a more unusual one: a picture of Saint Catherine and a kitten. The picture was beautiful; it was the gift of the Dominican Brothers at Woodchester. The kitten was a very handsome specimen.

"Perhaps," said Emily Fortey thoughtfully, "the spikes of Saint Catherine's wheel and the claws of the kitten are symbolic of our financial difficulties through which God wants us to love poverty."

In August, on the feast of Saint Lawrence, the little community made its first retreat. It was for only three days, but Father McNabb managed to get into those days a great variety of topics, as the careful notes taken by

Queenie Ellerker showed: instructions on faith, mortification, prayer, humility, obedience, the Presence of God, nature and grace, the love of God, the Church. Yet not one topic, as he handled it, was separate from the others; all formed a united whole of love and faith.

When the retreat ended, the group held its first council meeting, with Father McNabb, Queenie Ellerker, Emily Fortey and Anne McDiarmid present. At this meeting they decided to begin to call each other by the affectionate title of sister and their names as tertiaries, but this was to be done only among themselves. Queenie Ellerker became Sister Mary of the Blessed Sacrament, Emily Fortey and Anne McDiarmid became Sister Emily Catherine and Sister Anne Catherine.

The question of a costume was discussed and it was decided there be none for the present; each was to dress as she pleased. They decided, however, on certain religious observances and also to begin to chant the Divine Office chorally.

A little later another council meeting was held. At this one Father McNabb agreed to begin to give them instructions in the religious life. From Paris had come a copy of the Compendium of Constitutions which they were to study. Mrs. Perrins came to this meeting and, to the surprise of the others, asked to become an actual member of the community; she had said nothing about it previously even to her daughter, and she was joyously received by all present. When someone suggested that it was time to select one among them as head of the house, a vote was taken and Queenie Ellerker—by this time called by all of them Sister Mary, was elected. And at the same meeting Ethel, too, decided to join the community.

She took as a tertiary the name of Teresa Vincent, her mother that of Mary Magdalene.

During their first year at Corpus Christi there were many interested as well as interesting visitors. Miss Anstice Baker came from London often, proving herself a generous friend. She was so eager to see the community expand that she talked about it to everyone. It must grow very large, she said, for it was badly needed, and she was apt to grow annoyed when everyone did not immediately agree with her. To show how she felt about the little community at Leicester, she brought them a constantly increasing number of gifts—statues, food, a monstrance, as well as money. She also read several papers to lay groups assembled in the house, one on Joan of Arc and another on Savonarola.

Mabel Tothill, a well-known Quaker and a social worker, came to speak on the report of the Poor Law Commission and their own Anne McDiarmid spoke on the poetry of Cynewulf. The two women who called themselves Michael Field came to read from their own verse. Old London friends of Queenie Ellerker, they proved very popular to the Leicester people who came to hear them—Katherine, short, quick and witty, and Edith her niece, wistful and wan. Father McNabb called the latter "an elegant wasp, thinner than ever without her cowl." She had admitted to one group of those who came to hear her that at first she had been somewhat disappointed in the Church.

"I entered joyfully," she told them, "and then the dogmas crashed on me. I felt so shut up at times. I still do.

But always at the end of a long avenue I find Father McNabb, a door wide open."

It was interesting to note that Father McNabb, who had so many poetical and sometimes mystically inclined converts to his credit, always disavowed any such inclination for himself. "Thank God I've never had a vision," he said once. "I don't want them. The Apostles' Creed is good enough for me."

He hoped that they would soon receive permission to have the Blessed Sacrament in their house. "We hope," he said in one of his earlier talks to them, "that in a short time you will have His presence among you. That will make everything easier." But as yet the permission had not been secured.

Mrs. Perrins, whom the group of tertiaries called Sister Mary Magdalene, was the heart of Corpus Christi House, everyone agreed. The one trouble was that she wanted to be arms and willing feet for them all. She had to be restrained from too much cooking, too much cleaning. When in August several of the members were to be away for some weeks, they were troubled about the working proclivities of Sister Mary Magdalene, especially since she had grown increasingly less strong during the year. A letter was drafted to Ethel just before they left.

"Dear and honored Sister," it began, and went on to say that the writers of the letter would be away and might not be able to stay as long as was necessary unless they could obtain the services of a "competent and responsible person" who would prevent Sister Mary Magdalene "from undertaking the work of six women and three men all rolled in one and becoming ill in consequence."

Would Ethel take on herself this obligation? "Prostrate at your feet we beg you to remain in Leicester for the month of August," the letter ended. It was signed by the three who were to be away, and a pen-and-ink sketch of them prostrate on the floor was appended to the missive.

Ethel's reply was equally dignified. "Beloved and thrice honored Sisters," it began. "To your most humble request we willingly accede. We too are fully aware of the energies of the said Sister Mary Magdalene, amounting as you say to the energies of six women and three men. Double this number and you will have our own. These energies shall presently explode within the walls of our dwelling. Rise then, beloved Sisters, from your humble attitude, and return not till you have found seven others. Your unworthy sister and servant of the Torchbearing Hound.
                                                            Ethel."

# FOUR

By the second year's functioning of Corpus Christi House many activities were under way. The school, though small, was flourishing. The teachers became aware of the great need of more interesting material for children's reading. To a new magazine for children the Corpus Christi group were frequent contributors and the books for children by "Marie St. S. Ellerker" also increased in number.

In Holy Cross parish was a group of girls who wished to become Children of Mary, and Father McNabb suggested the Corpus Christi members take them in charge. They gladly agreed, held classes for them, gave them instruction on the Mass. They took the girls on visits to the church so that they could become familiar with its ornaments and learn the meaning and use of vestments and vessels. They taught them how to answer at Mass and how to prepare a sick person for the Sacraments.

Later this sodality was able to carry out all sorts of works for their church. They helped raise funds for a new edifice. They visited the sick and sometimes sat up all night with someone who had no nurse. They minded babies so that the mothers could go to Mass. They begged funds to buy a wheel chair in which a crippled girl could be brought to church. They produced a play to help the Brothers of St. Vincent de Paul with their charities. They collected clothing for the poor.

Sister Mary—as more and more Queenie Ellerker was being called by the people in Leicester—opened a class in church history, with especial emphasis on saints who had founded religious orders. The result produced by this class was to prove amazing. At the time there were no convents in the city and so these girls knew nothing at first hand about the religious life which they were now studying thoroughly. So interested did they become that eventually several of the group decided to enter religion. During the next eight years seventeen of the girls who had attended this class over the years became members of religious orders: Benedictines, Carmelites, Dominicans, Religious of the Cenacle, Little Sisters of the Poor, Visitation Sisters, and their own Corpus Christi congregation were all to benefit from these classes. Best of all, not one failed to persevere.

Corpus Christi House had other groups—a guild for juniors and one for girls who were in service in the city and who came to the house several times a month for instruction and then attended the church for Benediction.

There was a study club for adults where lectures were also given. One of these was on the history of the Poor Laws and visits were paid to the workhouse, the Labour Exchange, cottage homes for children, and homes for the sick poor.

During that year one more member of the Perrins family came to Corpus Christi. Mabel, the remaining daughter, joined the group and was given the community name of Sister Mary Paul. In that same autumn Sister Mary Magdalene was taken very ill, and the new member of the community nursed her. Father McNabb, who was devoted to his elderly tertiary, came to see her to say goodbye before he left for Rome to preach the Advent there and also to take his bachelor's examinations. He gave her his blessing and hoped she would be much better on his return.

"And you will pray for me, won't you?" he asked. "Especially during December for then I shall celebrate in Rome my silver anniversary."

The whole house was worried about Sister Mary Magdalene's precarious health. Before Christmas she suffered a severe heart attack. One of the Dominicans came to give her the last Sacraments. From Rome Father McNabb telegraphed his sympathy and prayers. The Bishop came to see her.

By Christmas she was better and the community arranged to have recreation and tea in her room on the holiday. The occasion would have been very happy had not Sister Mary Magdalene, propped up on pillows, looked so very wasted and thin.

She did not really ever recover fully and during the

next years she was to know much suffering. But her room was the one to which they all came for consolation. There they poured out joys and sorrows, and she comforted them. Not only her own community came to see her but many other people. Especially children came, among them some who knew that even if they were not wanted anywhere else, here they would receive a mother's love.

Once Father McNabb had said to her community, "Remember that next to having the Blessed Sacrament the greatest blessing is that of having an invalid who knows how to suffer well." They cherished this remark, for it was true that, despite their deep longing, they did not yet have the Treasure in their house. But they knew that they did have in their house what Father McNabb said was the next best.

On the feast of Saint Hilary he came to see them, full of stories about his stay in Rome, especially about his audience with Pius X which had been the highlight of it all. "His Holiness was so gracious to me," he said. "But do you know I had the most curious feeling while I was with him. He reminded me of myself. I was a little child at his feet and he treated me just as I would have treated a little child."

He smiled over one memory. "The Holy Father asked me where I came from and I said 'Anglia,' and he smiled and patted me on the head." Father McNabb felt of his head. "I can't bear to get a hair cut," he added.

He had come back to them on January 14, an auspicious day for the Corpus Christi members, for it was the third anniversary of the beginning of their work in Leicester, a work which they felt was his too.

He talked with them for a long time. He told them that

their work might go on or it might not; it was in the Lord's hands. The workers themselves had not, he thought, given much thought to this. They had been too busy. But what he liked best about them was the way in which they remained united in intention.

"I was struck while I was in Rome," he said, "by the extraordinary unity among the members of the Order and the great deal of freedom and brotherly love—not demonstrative but very real. It was a patient unity made up of almost conflicting interests. So on a morning like this we may become retrospective. We have gone on and things have been done. I have let the work develop. I have watched over it but I have not cared to initiate anything. I have however noted the astounding difficulties the members have overcome by going along in patience from day to day, living from hand to mouth, always feeling Our Lord has called them to their work. And so the words I take here for my text are very applicable: Sing joyfully to the Lord."

He said he had noted always this joy among them; that was why he used it as the text for his talk: "You and I don't know what His presence may mean in the months or days before us."

It was a consoling thing to reflect that it was God who had made them, that the Lord is God, he said, and told them the story of Cardinal Cajetan, a Dominican who was so bent in body that he was almost a hunchback. Once, when in Rome on some errand, Martin Luther saw him and made some jest about his appearance. The Cardinal said only in answer, "Ipse fecit nos et non ipsi sese."

"I think it is a great consolation," said Father McNabb,

"to think that we didn't have much to do with making ourselves. He made us and so we are more to Him than we are to ourselves. If we are crooked and ill made, it seems almost a want of delicacy to reproach Him."

He was happy to know that the little group at Corpus Christi looked on the Blessed Sacrament as the spring of all its work, practical as well as spiritual. He was happy to see how well they had done in these three years. With his usual humility he added that he often felt his own work among them had been done very poorly: "I have wished to be your brother here and often I have not been brotherly at all, and for that I wish to ask my sisters' pardon."

The talk had made a great impression on them all and from that time the motto "Serve the Lord with gladness" became a motto of theirs. Later several of the sisters chose the words to be engraved in their rings.

Sister Mary chose as her motto one suggested by Father McNabb especially for her. It was from the Gospel by Saint Luke and in the original Greek. It expressed the very opposite of the words of the rich man in the parable which told of the man who laid up treasure only for himself. These words expressed a very different way of life, and perhaps could be best expressed in English as spending oneself generously for God; literally translated they would be "rich towards God."

During the next few years the work of teaching went on and the Corpus Christi classes grew. But their work continued to branch out in new directions too. One was a general invitation the members extended to people to come and talk over matters about the Church, in order to interest further those with a slight interest in the Faith. No doubt the fact that all those at Corpus Christi House were converts was a great help. The women who came there were of all classes and of various sects, or none. Once a woman told them that for years she had gone to Mass in a Catholic church; she really wanted to become a Catholic but she was shy, and no one ever spoke to her or paid any attention to her; she was too timid to make the first advances. After hearing this story Sister Mary asked the girls in her Children of Mary group to make actual advances to any strangers among the women in their church.

Some people came merely out of curiosity to hear what these women had to say. As in any similar group, some came to learn and some came to argue. After a while the members of the house became very expert at this work. They learned that the poor and simple were easy to instruct; they were merely older children. The most difficult of all were the ritualistic Anglicans and in particular one woman who had for a time been an Anglican religious.

Sometimes they met with very pathetic cases among those whom the intellect did not hold back. One such was a woman who for some time had wished to enter the Church. She was all but ready when at an anti-Catholic lecture she heard the speaker tell of trap doors inside confessionals; after the confession the penitent was sometimes dropped through a door in the floor into a cell! The interesting thing was that this woman came to Corpus Christi anyway, evidently too far along on the road to conversion to stop, though it was clear she had half believed the lecturer.

Another woman said she could not understand about the Trinity. Being assured that she was not alone in this, she listened carefully to the teachings of the Church on the subject and then said, with an air of great relief, "Oh, you've made it very clear now. I didn't properly know there were three Gods." It was little wonder that after a few incidents like that Father McNabb insisted on a six months' attendance at Mass before he would examine a would-be convert.

Among the younger members who came to visit Corpus Christi House were some who had at various times attended a Sunday school, and their memories held fragments of what they had heard there. When the discussion was on sin, and one girl was asked what was Eve's sin, she gave a prompt answer. "She stole an apple."

"Do you remember how many sacraments there are?" asked Sister Emily. She didn't. "There are seven," said Sister Emily. "Do you remember the names of any of them?"

Again the girl shook her head, but this time she had a counter offer. "I can tell you the ten plagues of Egypt though."

The sisters were very patient with them all, for they were in earnest despite their ignorance. They never asked foolish or malicious questions, and their ignorance was innocent. Many of them were girls who worked all day and gave up their evenings to come to these instruction groups.

Part of the success of the work was no doubt due to the fact that Father McNabb stressed that they must never approach instruction from a controversial viewpoint; they must remember always that their first duty was to try to understand the point of view of those who came to them. He urged them to make use of any opening offered to present God's truth, and this they faithfully tried to do.

One very successful effort was the staging on successive Christmases of Monsignor Benson's very charming play of the Nativity. The hall in which it was produced was the property of the Unitarians and most of the audience was Protestant. The players felt greatly repaid for their work when after one performance a non-Catholic woman told them she had never thought of the Virgin Mary as being like that. "Wasn't she lovely—and wasn't she brave," she said admiringly.

Perhaps the most interesting of all the work they engaged in during these first years was that of aiding the Motor Chapels. This was something very new at the time. It was the brain child of Father Herbert Vaughan, a member of a family to which English Catholics owed a great deal, and who was at the time head of the Catholic Missionary Fathers. He knew that work was being done in the cities to acquaint people with the Faith, and that it was needed. But he wanted to send helpers on the highways far from the cities, to seek the lost sheep who had no one to hunt for them, to take the Faith to those who had no knowledge of it or whose information was distorted, to put the truth before people who had heard of the Catholic Church only from those who hated her.

Miss Anstice Baker, well known among London social workers, was at the head of a band of women who helped these priests. She asked the sisters at Corpus Christi to aid her in the work. She and her helpers promised to take care of all expenses; what they wanted from the sisters was their time.

The program had been carefully worked out. Someone went in advance to a little town and rented a hall where a lecture could be given. Then posters were put up and leaflets advertising the lecture series were left, whenever possible, at each house so that the invitations would be made more personal. What was very amazing to the chapel workers was the polite way in which they were welcomed and the promises made to come to the lectures. There were many places—Dereham, Wymondham, Baldock, Stevenage, Fowey, Sea View—where the motor chapels went. They had a powerful effect, both immediate and in the future, for in some places new parishes rose from these visits. And the traveling missionaries made many friends.

Baldock had proved especially interesting, for there they found a community of French nuns, whose work in their native France had been visiting prisons; this group had cared for those at the well known St. Lazare prison in Paris. When religious congregations were exiled from their home land, the sisters had come with some of their students and settled in the little English village. Not one could speak English and they welcomed Sister Mary with joy when they found she could not only understand them but could speak their own language well—"like a native" they told her admiringly. They said they were earning a living by doing fine laundry and that people liked their work. But to the people of the village this group and its convent life were a thing mysterious. It was clear that they wanted to be friendly but were a little uneasy about this French colony in their very British village.

The Motor Corps method was to pull up the chapel car in a field and there have Mass said each morning. What Catholics there were in the village assisted; some who had been long away from the sacraments or who had been outside the Church for years often returned to their duties. At certain hours the car was left open and people came to examine it and to talk and take with them Catholic Truth literature. Always before they left, the workers talked on the Faith and the Sacraments and urged their visitors to come to the lectures which the Fathers gave evenings.

Once an anti-Catholic lecturer followed the car from Baldock to Stevenage and on to Buntingford. It was a night when Monsignor Benson, who lived in that town, was to speak. He had proved a wonderful addition to their staff of lecturers for he spoke in simple analogies to the people listening. God, he would say, often uses fellow beings to aid us. For instance, though we ask God for our daily bread, we do not hesitate to go to the bakeshop for it, nor think it derogatory to God to do so. "We do not expect God to interfere directly in the matter of our morning roll," he said, "and so it is too in the spiritual world." And from that amusing beginning the Monsignor was able to speak more easily to his Protestant listeners on the touchy subject of confession.

That there was an organized opposition following them from town to town became clear from some of the questions found in the box. "Why have you come to a place where you are not wanted?" they found more than once and phrased in different ways. Some of the queries were too pretentious to have been thought out by the audiences to whom they spoke. They were meant to impress the listeners of course and make them feel it would be hard for these strangers to match the villagers' intellectual capacities.

One night a learned psychologist from London, the speaker of the evening, pulled out a very complicated question. He read it aloud and then said he would try to answer it so that all could understand him. Then he went into a deep and learned disquisition on the matter, so deep that even the priests were impressed. Next day it was learned that his remarks had made an even deeper impression on the people of the village.

"It's like Baron de Vaux in *The Talisman*," said the highly amused Monsignor Benson. "Remember how impressed he was by the Bishop's explanation, and especially, he said, because he hadn't understood a word of it."

As for the question submitted which wanted to know why the missionary group had come to Huntingford, this was read aloud by Father Vaughan, who then looked around at the crowded hall and said courteously that it was evident the lectures were not proving unwelcome. He had, in fact waited a whole week to begin them, during which time he had paid for the rent of the hall. He had delayed his own lectures because Protestants from several towns were holding a conference and he had not wanted to interfere with their sessions.

It was perhaps unfortunate that the Protestant lecturer heard this answer and said it was a lie. Next day several of the town's Protestants came to Father Vaughan to ask for proof of what he had said and he handed them the receipted bill for the use of the hall. They went promptly to the opposition lecturer and asked him to apologize. When he refused to do so, he was denied the use of benches taken from the hall to another building where he planned to speak at the same time and in refutation of Monsignor Benson. The chapel car missionaries were very happy about this for their audience had greatly increased and some people had had to stand up. Now there would be room for all to sit as well as to listen.

The priests had said nothing unkind about anyone, including the lecturer, who had certainly been very rough toward his opponent. Some young men in the village were so incensed by this they demanded a retraction or otherwise threatened a ducking in the canal. Extra police were provided for that evening but the lecturer chose the better part and took a train for London. The Motor Corps ended in peace a highly successful mission.

At almost every town the Salvation Army came in a body, and not to scoff. After the lectures they remained to discuss the subject of the lecture further. What amazed the chapel car group was the fact that these men and women seemed to grasp the idea of confession, of satisfaction and mortification better than any sect with which they had come in touch.

Perhaps it was the children who gave the Corpus Christi workers their greatest joy. At Fowey they could find no flowers to decorate the altar and some small boys who were hanging around heard of this. Why were flowers important, they wanted to know. Sister Mary explained that one wanted to offer to God in the Blessed Sacrament —and she showed them the altar at which they gazed with respectful surprise—all the world held of beauty. The boys departed but hours later they came back, their arms full of honeysuckle which they had climbed the cliffs to get. "Here," said one, "these are for your Blessed Sacrament."

Next to the children the old people were a delight. Once Sister Mary came across a very old woman in a tiny cottage. She welcomed her visitor with courtesy and was happy to talk with her. Sister Mary realized the old woman was too lame to come to a meeting but it was evident that she was delighted to have a visitor with whom to chat. But she shook her head sadly when she learned that Sister Mary was a Catholic.

"I wish, dear, you could have loved the Lord Jesus too," she said. "But I suppose you can't. You have to worship the Virgin, don't you?"

There was only love and sympathy in the wrinkled face. Sister Mary assured her that she did love Jesus too, and with a love which she and her fellow Catholics gave to no one but Him, not even to His mother. She talked to the absorbed old woman about the many churches built to shelter Him in the Blessed Sacrament, about men and women who gave their lives to His service, about the Catholic belief that He was with His people in the churches and on the altars.

When Sister Mary rose to go the old hands held hers tightly. "You'll come back, won't you, dear?" she begged. "And then we'll talk together more about the love of Jesus."

When later Sister Mary was telling the story to Father McNabb, she added, "and all the way home I thought of how that would be a much more fruitful subject to discuss with our separated brethren than the ones they and we too are more apt to choose."

"How right you are," said Father McNabb. "I'm afraid

we don't always use the persuasive way. We show them the grand—and I am afraid sometimes fearsome spiritual machinery of the Church when people ought to be speaking of the love of God and His mercy."

# FIVE

IN NOVEMBER OF 1913 THE CORPUS CHRISTI COMMUNITY moved once more. They could have asked for no better house than the one they were now to occupy nor for a better location. It was on property which belonged to the Dominicans. It was a fine large house and that meant they would be able greatly to increase their activities. The place was quiet too, in the New Walk, where vehicular traffic was not permitted. It was shaded by great trees and had a fine garden.

Best of all it was next to the priory church of Holy Cross. Since the sisters did not yet have the Blessed Sacrament in their house, it was a joy to be so near. In fact, from some of their windows they could see the sanctuary lamp flickering on the altar.

As soon as they were established in the new home, a

council meeting was held. Among other things they decided that, the Bishop permitting, the members would begin to wear some kind of distinguishing costume. They had worked in secular dress for five years now; it was time to assume uniform wear.

They chose a white dress with wide pleats and a belt, a short black veil with a white band on the forehead, and a black cloak to wear outdoors. At the singing of the Office they would also wear the long white scapular which showed they were daughters of Saint Dominic. At the waist they wore a rosary and around their neck on a silver chain replicas of the medal which Sister Mary had been wearing since they had been in Leicester.

The new work which they now hoped to take up was that of retreats. They turned to the Jesuit Father Plater for training in this for he was known as an enthusiastic planner of retreats. In the Nottingham diocese these were quite unknown to the people and therefore the Bishop was keenly interested in this new project. In January of 1914 it was decided that the Corpus Christi House would be one of the retreat houses which Father Plater called his "spiritual power stations."

The Corpus Christi group was by that time well established in Leicester and had more members. The year before they moved to New Walk they had given to Bishop Brindle the results of a year's work: 26 converts, 80 under instruction, 3 lapsed Catholics brought back to the Church, 12 prepared for baptism. In addition to this there were the weekly classes, the convert instruction classes, a confirmation class, frequent lectures to special groups, in addition to the work of teaching.

In the line of social service work it was usually Sister Emily who took the leading part. Father McNabb said she was adding to her title of spouse of Christ that of guardian of the poor. She was a member of the Leicester health council, the Personal Service League, the Society for the Prevention of Cruelty to Children, the Catholic Social Guild. She sometimes gave talks at the house on subjects such as woman in the home, housing problems, nursery homes.

Anne McDiarmid eventually left them during those years. She had gone to teach with the Dominicans at Stone and there she remained. Those she had left would always miss her, not for the money she had contributed but for the intellectual wealth she gave so generously. To watch her instructing young people had been a joy. She never hurried. She considered each person as an individual. She was able to transmit her ardent faith to the hearts of her listeners.

Of the gradually growing little group at Corpus Christi House it was Sister Mary Magdalene who helped more than anyone with her prayers and the affection she gave to all who came to her room, for, since she had become something of an invalid after her heart attack, most of her efforts emanated from that room.

The others of the group were the active members. At the head of them all was the indefatigable Sister Mary in whose hands lay the success or failure of the whole project, who managed the house, went with the motor missionaries, and also wrote books. There were also many visitors to entertain, for word of Corpus Christi House had spread and many came to examine its work. Bishop

Brindle came to give advice and to admire their efforts. Bishop Keating came and Bishop Burton of Clifton and Father Couteurier, the well-known Dominican, who said Mass in Sister Mary Magdalene's room. Old friends like the Michael Fields came, and so did many new friends. Corpus Christi House was a busy place.

The intention to open the house to retreats had at first daunted the group. There were certain disadvantages they must face. There was no Blessed Sacrament in their chapel. Even though there was seclusion from traffic in their new home and the garden was private, there would be no opportunity for the long walks which were supposedly a part of the power station retreats. Then too the house was very simply furnished, for the community had little money to spend on furniture. But the chief difficulty was that the work was new to them. They were a little dismayed at what they had undertaken.

They need not have worried. From the beginning the new work went so well that they began to wonder if perhaps retreats could not fail. Father Plater had warned them not to be troubled if at first only a few people came. And it was true that only six women attended the first, given by Father Wylie. But of the six—one, an author of some repute, was not long afterwards received into the Church and she said it was this retreat which had made her take the final step.

A Jesuit, Father Rickey, gave the next retreat. He was a man of gentle speech and winning manner. Of the girls who made it, four were soon afterwards to enter religion. It was little wonder the sisters felt encouraged to go on.

One day several boys came to Sister Mary to say they

had decided the girls were getting all the attention and they were being left out in the cold. What about a retreat for them? She promised to see that they had one and suggested they form a committee of their own to make the arrangements. Meantime she asked Father Bede Jarrett if he would act as retreat master. However, knowing the ways of boys and fearing most of them might not come at all, she asked him what was the smallest number for which he would consider it worth while coming. The answer came promptly on a postcard: "One. I don't think I could come for less than that."

The number who came proved a real reward to the anxious sisters—twenty boys. It was a fine retreat, for Father Jarrett had the wonderful quality of not speaking over the boys' heads or treating them like children.

Father McNabb came to preach a retreat for university women and gave a brilliant series of talks. "He satisfies the intellect and appeals to the heart," said one of the retreatants to Sister Mary, who felt it summed up their Father Vincent in one sentence.

He had told the women that they were assembled "to hear God's point of view—one of the means of detaching yourself from your own point of view." He spoke of silence—"that most crowded thing. I speak and you listen. But silence is often more intellectual than speech. It is a greater display of energy of soul. If this retreat helps you in nothing else, may it make your souls grow in that central activity which is called Prayer with God."

Once, at a meeting where the discussion was about the increasing difficulties with boys and girls whose home life and training was far from good, the suggestion was made that a retreat be offered to non-Catholics as one way of helping to a common understanding of Catholic effort and method. The secretary of the local Y.M.C.A. and the mayor of the city were present and both thought it an excellent idea. Sister Mary, who had made the suggestion, had not really thought that her challenge would actually be taken up, but it was, and the never failing Father McNabb was asked to be retreat master for the six men who volunteered.

It was, the community agreed, the most unusual retreat ever given at Corpus Christi House, and Father McNabb said he had never worked so hard at one either. After each talk, he was besieged with questions, and it took long ringing of bells before the questions stopped or the answers either, for both sides were enjoying themselves too much to think about food.

The men carried out all the retreat demands, keeping silence in the refectory and listening closely to the reading —John Ascough's *French Windows.* Weeks later one of the retreatants met Sister Mary and told her, "We've been talking about that retreat ever since. We had the time of our lives and we think your Father McNabb is wonderful."

It was a great sorrow to the community at Leicester, as well as to many other people in the city, when in 1914 Father McNabb was made prior of the house at Hawksyard, near London. He too was sorry to leave this group to whom he had been spiritual director, adviser, retreat master—everything.

On his first return visit he told Sister Mary how much he wished he were back in Leicester; he found his newer duties very heavy. "But of course a superior must not merely support the Rule. He must be the Rule in flesh and blood. I don't know that I ever felt my shortcomings so much as since this new priorship has been placed on me," he said. Then he sighed. "But you and I are here in authority by God's will. We are not here to do our own will, not even under the subtle self-deception that it is God's will. Oh, what a self-emptying way is His!"

Then he talked of the community whose life had been bound with his for some years. "It is a kind of recurring marvel to me that people have faith in me and are so perplexingly loyal," he said. "But your little community has been loyal with a devotion almost too great. I cannot recall a trivial deed or chance word which has hindered my work, or a thought in your mind which has not been directed toward furthering my poor efforts for the Master's honor."

Sister Mary said nothing. Her heart was too full to let her speak. He was looking at her very soberly. "Too often I have shirked burdens and laid them on you," he said sadly. "Too often I have been heedless of the sacrifices you were over-willing to bear."

She shook her head and tried to find words to answer him. With that abrupt way he had of trying to turn anything from himself, he said suddenly that he had never really thanked the sisters for the farewell gift they gave him when he left in April. But Sister Mary was remembering his first letter to her after he had gone; it was a gift better than any they could have given him.

"I leave you," he had written, "in the conviction that now at last you will have the chance of growth. Your hopes are heavier. The blessing has come through my withdrawal. God bless you and all you do," and then had come one of his self-depreciating and humble confessions:

"I have asked and obtained from you more sacrifices probably than anyone in the Church."

Sister Mary had interesting information to give him. Some of the community had gone several times to the outlying areas of Leicester to talk and to teach catechism. As was their custom they asked at each house if there were any Catholics there. They had found many in Aylestone, some entirely lapsed, some who had never had any sacrament save baptism and many of the children had not even had that.

Sunday after Sunday the sisters came there and in a room above the village bakery held a sort of Sunday school. The children came eagerly and before long many had been baptized. It was not that the parents had been unwilling, but no one had come to ask them; no one had seemed interested in these lambs of the flock.

When a priest came to say Mass there he made the electrifying discovery that this would be the first Mass to be said in Aylestone since the days of the Reformation when it had been forbidden.

"We felt we were very definitely preparing the way of the Lord there," one of the sisters wrote later. "We managed to make the bare room look a little like a chapel. We succeeded in getting together all the articles needed. And we even trained a very hastily put together choir."

A friend had given them a beautiful French doll to raffle off in Leicester, Sister Mary told Father McNabb. With the proceeds they were able to buy a chalice. When everything was ready and the first Mass said, the sisters had the joy of knowing that forty-one people came and more than half received Communion. Aylestone was back in the Catholic fold.

She told him that their work there had its pathetic stories and its humorous ones as well. The children were apt to produce unexpected answers to some of the questions, as the small boy who held up his hand importantly when the question was asked: "How many sacraments are there?"

"Please Sister," he called out, "there's seven—six for ladies and seven for gentlemen."

Sister Mary Magdalene was too much of an invalid to be active on these missions or for the retreats, but she followed them closely in her prayers. Sister Emily said of her that "only in Heaven shall we know all we owe to her prayers and her unselfishness, and what these have done for the community."

At the end of missions it was to her room that they came to tell what had taken place; it was her prayers which sustained them while they were away. It was to her welcoming smile, her eager interest that they returned.

It was during the retreats that Sister Mary Magdalene proved very valuable. Girls and women who were making them came to see her and to pour out to her their hopes and sorrows, things they could tell no one else. Over a cup of tea more than one problem found a solution. As for the children, it was hard to keep them from Sister Magdalene's room; they loved her and were with difficulty torn away.

She thoroughly enjoyed hearing about one retreat which Father Plater had organized for nineteen boys. All were finished with school but had not yet found work. He never left his retreatants. He slept in the house, ate with the boys, joined in their recreation. He invited them to come to his room at any time they wished and the room was never empty save for the few hours he gave to sleep. It was a very successful retreat. Like Father McNabb, he had a way with boys.

After the First World War broke over England, many things changed, and among them the work of the Corpus Christi Sisters. All the religious organizations, utterly unprepared for the demands made upon them, worked to provide the soldiers, first of all, with chaplains. The Y.M.C.A. had thousands of cards printed, each to be filled out by the enlisted men: what was their church affiliation? If they were not in touch with it, would they like to be? The cards of those who filled them in by saying that they were Catholics were very courteously sent to the Catholic authorities.

One day Father Plater came to ask Sister Mary if he could count on her and her sisters to go through these cards and classify them. He had been the first to take up this work but found himself overwhelmed with its mass. It would clearly be impossible for one man to handle it, and every priest was busy, much too busy to help him. This the sisters were happy to do and when he came to thank them, he had a second request to make: would they form a correspondence group for Catholic soldiers?

Four thousand letters were sent out, each with a personal message from one of the sisters to a soldier. The response to this gesture was amazing. It was clear that nearly everyone had answered; it was also clear that many others had heard about it and were sending in their names. Obviously the men were happy to get a personal word meant just for them, and their letters gave the sisters one sad reflection: it was pathetic to find how grateful these men were for the small gift of a letter.

"You letter has done me as much good as going to Mass when you can't get to go," wrote one. "I'll remember you wherever I go. Good night, Sister, and God bless you." And one letter said, "You can't imagine how glad I was to get your letter. It is the first one I've ever had in my life." When they looked up his record, they found he had been brought up in an orphan asylum. Often the letters were full of little stories of home and their own people; fathers would list the names and ages of their children and the school they attended.

The soldiers had also been asked if there was anything they would like sent to them. Many asked for religious books so that they could better explain to their Protestant comrades something of their faith. One interesting thing was to note that many had evidently read and enjoyed the stirring novels of Monsignor Benson and wanted copies; there were hundreds of these requests. One other request was for cigarettes, but these were few compared to those for books. But the chief request in almost every answer was for another letter.

One young soldier wrote that he was a Catholic; he knew he was one and that was all. The chaplain kept asking him about going to his duties. "I would go soon enough if I knew how," he wrote. "I don't like to ask the busy priest for he is too busy as it is." One lad wrote that for some reason he had always written Roman Catholic when he was asked what was his religion. That was how he got his name on their list. After an exchange of letters he asked, "Is there any way of becoming a proper member of your church?" and within months he had become the proper member he wanted to be.

Sometimes the sisters helped with love affairs. One soldier wrote begging them to send a letter to his young lady: "I trust you, Sister, to keep her true to me for she is awfully pretty." And one sister, called to the parlor, found one of her correspondents there with a girl.

"This is my young lady, Sister," he introduced her. "I want you to change her religion for me please."

Even before the war the sisters had been more than once disturbed by the unhappy home conditions in the lives of many boys and girls. They had taken up the work of helping with delinquent children when a civil committee was formed in Leicester. One of the sisters became a member of the committee. Their own work was, they found, best carried out through scouts and girl guides. Soon they were deep in Brownies and Cubs as well as with the older groups. In fact, their troop of Girl Guides was the first in Leicester and one of the first in the country.

After the war began the Corpus Christi members extended this work to London where two women, Mrs. Kensington and Lady Philip Gibbs, rented a house where young people could make retreats. They hoped to help all young people from very small ones to boys who now had to leave school and become family wage earners.

Among the members sent to work at the London house was Gertrude Johnson who acquired considerable fame as leader and best friend of the Wolf Cubs. She and her sister Teresa had come to the house recently and on August 15, 1917, she was professed as a Dominican tertiary in the London house by Father McNabb. Despite the exigencies of war and the demands on everyone's time, it was made a lovely ceremony.

Father McNabb took as his text the verses in St. John about Mary and Martha. Sister Gertrude, he said, was choosing the better part. He spoke of the feast day as one very specially associated with Saint Dominic for it was on that day that his first disciples had made their profession.

"At first it was not quite easy to see why this particular place in Scripture was chosen as the gospel reading for this feast. But second thoughts show how the Mother of God is personified by Mary and Martha and so they typify the type consecrated to God. We see that Our Blesed Lady was neither Mary nor Martha but both—something in her of Mary, the type of the purely contemplative life; something of Martha, the type of the active life."

He looked at the people before him and went on. "But there is a life higher than either. It is the apostolic life, the blending of both. It is the form of religious life renewed by Saint Dominic in the Church."

He spoke sadly of the way in which the war had sent apostles to the trenches and emptied the novitiates. "A greater call will be made on women to take the place of men and do the work which wants doing, and women will meet the demand. If we have a minute knowledge of the Incarnation, it is through Our Lady; she taught the apostles; she spent her last years in teaching."

He gave the ring and the scapular to Sister Gertrude after he had blessed them. It was the one profession ceremony carried out at the London house.

On the same day, Sister Mary Magdalene was elected superior of the house in Leicester. This left Sister Mary free to help with the greatly increasing work of retreats at the London house as well as at the house in Leicester. It gave her time to train a group of young sisters and to write articles. Later these were to be made into books. She would write them chapter by chapter to the young sisters and ask their advice regarding changes. *Master Where Dwellest Thou?* and *Saint Dominic,* written for children, were printed during these years.

Besides the sorrows which the bitter war had brought, the Corpus Christi community had suffered, in 1916, a personal loss. Sister Teresa Vincent, who had been Ethel Perrins, died. For three months she fought the tuberculosis which was draining her life away. The hospital authorities had loaned the community a consumptive's hut and it was placed in the garden near the house. There her sister nursed her day and night. Their mother was too much of an invalid to leave the house. Sister Mary went from one to the other, trying also to keep up with the school and household and faced always with the coming separation from her beloved little sister.

Sister Teresa Vincent made her vows on Corpus Christi day with Father McNabb and Father Bull beside her. She died during the octave. She had been early in her short life a postulant in the Carmelite Order and so had taken the name of Teresa in her later affiliation. She was laid to rest in the cemetery at Hawksyard and later, when Father McNabb visited her grave, he wrote to the sisters at Leicester, "What a quiet place for sleep! Yet she sleeps only to the sorrows of this life. Her sleep is but a fuller life in God."

Some months before her young sister's illness and death,

Sister Mary had herself been in danger; the doctors were afraid of a lung affliction for which they knew no cure. She did recover, however, and the doctor who had cared for her expressed his surprise; he said he had not treated her long enough to be able to say it was due to his efforts. But some time after Ethel's death a note was found in her purse: she had offered herself to God. She was ready to die if her sister Queenie was left alive to carry on their work.

Sister Mary Magdalene was able to carry out her duties as superior, even though shortly after Ethel's death she became completely an invalid. She left her room but rarely and after some time was all but confined to her bed. She lived her life in her room, a pleasant one, one of whose windows overlooked Holy Rosary Church. At night she could see the light on the altar. It kept watch with her through nights of pain when she could not sleep. But her sisters said she had another window and they called it "our anchoress window." It was the window of her soul and from it shone her love of God and brought light to the many people who visited her.

She carried out the duties of superior well, but it was her prayer life which was of greatest importance. Her prayers went everywhere, to the battlefields of France, to the little mission in the great city, to religious and priests everywhere. Often the teaching sisters brought to her room some small child, come for her first day at school and very frightened. Sister Mary Magdalene sent them away smiling after a talk and a sweet and a little prayer. Grown people came with their troubles and after some conversation and the inevitable cup of tea at her bedside, they came away feeling better. The little room was in all truth a sanctuary.

In the early autumn of 1917, when armies were worn out and civilians without number had been killed, Pope Benedict XV issued a proclamation: he wished all practising Catholics, old and young, to make their Communions on July 16, the feast of Our Lady of Carmel, with the intention that peace come soon. Especially he hoped that all children would take part in processions of intercession for peace on that day.

In many parts of England his wish was carried out. Corpus Christi at Leicester had a fine procession. But perhaps the sisters at the London house saw the most memorable celebration of all.

The feast fell on a Sunday. The procession of children was to start from Westminster Cathedral in the afternoon. Pavements, windows, roofs around the square were crowded. Small boys and girls in white with bright banners marched importantly along the main line of the procession. They had come from the suburbs and even from other cities and, as they marched along, the children sang hymns and recited the rosary and the litany of Our Lady. After the long ranks of children had filed past, came the confraternities with their banners, the clergy, bishops, and last of all Cardinal Bourne. By that time everyone was singing.

"It must have reached Heaven," wrote Sister Gertrude to the house at Leicester.

All traffic had been stopped for blocks around. When the procession returned to the cathedral square, the little children filed into the open space. A high platform had been built and from this the Cardinal gave Benediction of the Blessed Sacrament. Then the crowd dispersed.

It was that very evening that the first break came. The Allies had pushed back the opposing armies for the first time and the newsboys were shouting, "Big victory for the Allies." Those who were moved by hearing this news, coming so soon after the great procession for peace, felt too that, though the war might go on for some time more, a great spiritual victory had been gained that day.

# *SIX*

Sister mary magdalene had cherished one great dream during her eleven years of life in religion: to become a missionary in foreign lands. Even now, in her days of invalidism, she held that dream. Sometimes the thought came to her that she might get better. She might be well enough to go herself. And, even if she could never go herself, perhaps some day her community would be asked to work in some other country.

In 1918, when the war was all but over, the request she had hoped for came. From Port of Spain in Trinidad, British West Indies, came a letter from the Dominican Archbishop there. Could a few of the community at Leicester come to work in his island archdiocese, Archbishop Dowling wrote to ask.

To the community it seemed a wonderful offer, a wonderful opportunity. It also seemed a bit mad perhaps even to consider, with their small numbers, splitting the group. Even yet there were hardly enough members to fill one house and lend a few to the house in London.

There was no slightest hesitation because of such unimportant reasons. Sister Mary accepted for her community and promised to send three members the following year. But from the day the letter went to the Archbishop the preparation began. Sister Mary Magdalene helped all she could, saying nothing of her own hope that somehow she might get well enough to go with them. Meantime she read up on the place where the new mission was to begin its work, its history and how and when it became a Christian land. As she read she shared her information with the others. By the time the three were ready to leave, they were a very well instructed group on the historical, physical and spiritual facts of their future home.

Trinidad was discovered by Columbus on his third voyage to the New World and was named by him for the Holy Trinity whom he had invoked for much of the difficult sailing. The ships had been becalmed under a burning sun, their drinking water was all but gone, their food all but spoiled by the tropical heat. Therefore when an island was sighted by his rejoicing crew, Columbus gratefully gave it the name La Trinidad.

He came there in peace, as he had on his other exploratory voyages, and the Indians trusted him. Those who came after him to the island were not so gentle towards the men they found there; after that first peaceful coming, history's pages recorded dark violence and crime. The

Indians, who had met later comers as they had Columbus and his men, were robbed and some were taken away as slaves. Hate of the Spaniards exploded and some of the adventurers were killed. For a time no white man came to the island.

Then two Dominican priests decided to go there to try to convert the Indians. They were well received, for it was apparent they came unarmed and for no hostile reason. The Indians listened to their instruction and a considerable number were converted. Then, while the missionaries were still there, a Spanish ship came into the harbor. The natives were frightened, and with good reason. This ship had guns mounted on her deck and the Indians remembered what had happened earlier to their people. However, it was felt that the missionaries would afford them protection and would explain to the white men that these Indians were peaceful people. So they went unsuspectingly to the ship, lured by offers of beads and cheap trinkets. They did not return, for as soon as they were on board, the ship weighed anchor and sailed away, taking the Indians with them.

The first reaction of those left behind was to kill the two Spanish missionaries, for they suspected they were in the plot. The priests were, in the meantime, trying to get those Indians who had been stolen returned to Trinidad, for among them were the chief of the island and his wife, both of them Christians. The Indians agreed to wait, but time went by and no one returned. The Indians held a council and the missionaries were put to death. The tribe then formally renounced Christianity as being a deceitful and cruel religion.

Two hundred years passed. Other missionaries came

there and were martyred in their turn, for the memory of their betrayal remained with the Indians. Then the Dutch came and the French and English buccaneers, but none of them found the precious metals for which they were all searching so covetously. The island was still considered to be Spanish territory but in a war between France and Spain the island was in 1802 formally given to England. Since then it had been a Crown colony.

This much they learned from Sister Mary Magdalene's reading. For practical information they must wait until the travelers sent back word of what they had found. Sister Mary had planned to go with them to establish the foundation but at the last moment Sister Mary Magdalene was taken so ill that she could not leave her, and remained to nurse her. The sick woman felt deep regret that she was the cause of preventing Sister Mary from going with the others, but most of all she regretted that she could not go herself. "The mother of holy ambitions," the others called her affectionately.

In October of 1919 the little band of three sailed, Sister Josephine at their head. Sister Mary went with them as far as she could, right to the gates of the dock where a launch took them to a steamer riding at anchor some distance out in the river. As they took their seats in the launch and it chugged away, the departing three saw waving at them Sister Mary who had somehow managed to get past the gate and was staying as long as she could and as close as possible to her daughters.

"The trinity to the island of the Trinity," as Father McNabb had named them, had a long trip and a very rough one. But they were good sailors and the two weeks trip was not too unpleasant, they wrote in their first letter home.

On the very day they reached their mission, Sister Mary Magdalene died. The others were all around her when Father Ball came to give her the last Sacraments. Past her window, in the church of Holy Cross, one could see the flicker of the light which had so often comforted her when she was wakeful and in pain. A few days before her death she said to Sister Mary, "I am dying sooner than I wanted to," and what she meant was clear.

She was buried beside her daughter in the lovely little cemetery of the Dominican Fathers at Hawksyard, and it was Father McNabb who said the last prayers over her. The little group of her community stood beside him.

It had been a dreary November day but, when the words of death and life were spoken over her, the weather was changing. The wind had died down and only a slight breeze moved the evergreens. A light fall of snow sparkled in the sunlight as the white robed Dominicans and the sisters in their white dresses and black veils walked slowly from the grave. Now they had two praying for them in Heaven.

When the Corpus Christi Sisters left England the day had been cold and dreary. It was a very different climate which greeted them when from their steamer they saw the lovely bays and the rocky entrance of Trinidad, its palm trees and sunshine. They had been told that the Archbishop would come to meet them, and it was a comfort to them to know that once again they would be guided in their work by a Dominican.

When the launch reached the landing, a crowd was

waiting for them, both cleric and lay among them. They were taken directly to the convent of the Sisters of St. Joseph of Cluny. They did not have time to be homesick, as Sister Josephine wrote home, because they were at home.

Archbishop Dowling had given them a convent which was to be the first Corpus Christi house in the mission field and which, they were happy to find, was almost in the shadow of Holy Rosary Church, another link with home for it was in the charge of Dominicans. The sisters were to have charge of the Spaccapietra Home for the Aged, which had a chapel and also contained a greatly loved shrine dedicated to Saint Anthony. Best of all, the Blessed Sacrament was in the tabernacle there.

Despite the friendly welcome, it took some weeks for the sisters to become assimilated to the great change in the way of living and the people. This was a colorful place to which they had come and a colorful people. Little brown skinned children came shyly up to them, their big eyes full of curiosity about these white clad women. Old creole women with beautifully starched white dresses with long trains, bright turbans and loaded with heavy jewelry, smiled at them as they passed; on their heads were big baskets of fruit and vegetables which they were on their way to sell in the markets.

On the sea were boats manned by men with long poles who were taking their produce to incoming steamers. Not one nation was represented there, but many—most of them Negroes, but there were also many others. In the streets were Hindus selling oranges and in the shops were smiling Chinese merchants. Most fascinating to the newcomers from the north were the street cries—"piment, peppa, cucumba"—"plantain for the Papa, pumpkin for the Babee"—"Fee-ee-sh," this cry going up a whole octave on the scale in the one syllable.

On the debit side were some of the most unpleasant forms of life they had ever met, not least the huge cockroaches and spiders which came from nowhere and seemed actually, to the alarmed sisters, to be advancing to attack them. Also there was the great heat, a contrast to England's gentle warmth. They became acclimated, however, and they learned not to run from the Gulliver-sized insects but to subdue them with a broom.

They could not have asked for more kindness and fellowship than that with which they met. A few days after they were settled in their convent, a gift came from the Archbishop: an oil stove with an oven—"in case you might like to make cakes," ran his note. And on the same day a little old creole woman came with a gift for the sisters —a piece of sugared cocoanut for each. She invited them to visit her and pointed out her tiny cabin on a hill, with a palm tree in front of it and at the back a cotton tree full of snowy balls.

Corpus Christi Sisters, Father McNabb was wont to say, were a restless lot, always wanting to improve something. This trait showed itself in the Trinidad missionaries who set to work to make life happier for the old people entrusted to their care.

Some of their charges had seen better days and had owned property; now they were alone and poor with no one to care for them, friendless and homeless. Some were old family servants whom their employers had placed there because they were too old to work; these old people were often visited by their former employers and by the grown-ups whom they had tended as children.

The food provided for the old people was plentiful but, as Sister Josephine put it, unimaginative. The sisters wanted to be able to give them something more interesting occasionally. First they decided to have what in England was known as a Pound Day. They asked people to bring them on that day a pound of food of some kind.

The Archbishop was the first to respond, and with a fine square of sugared cake. The sisters had placed in the visitor's room a large sheet to hold the offerings, and all day long these came. Little white children, delicate as so often are those who live in the tropics, brought pounds of rice and coffee and sugar. Little colored children, with not much to give, brought cocoanuts. One very old man, a stevedore, came with four penny loaves as his contribution. A tiny colored boy brought, in a small screwed up bit of paper, a farthing's worth of salt. One of the first things the sisters learned at Port of Spain was that if you asked you received.

In the evening, when they put away the offerings, they were amazed at the generosity and realized that the boast of Trinidad was no idle one: no one would ever starve there, for some one would find the hungry one and bring help, whether to a sick old man or a little child who needed home and love.

In front of the big stone house built on the shore of the Dry River ran a long cloister, and there the old ladies sat in the shadowed coolness. The hospice had no wards but a series of small rooms, each opening on the shady porch. There was no common dining room and the sisters planned to open one, only to find that their guests

71

objected to taking their meals in one large room. The idea was given up.

One thing the cloisters lacked, the sisters decided, was plants and flowers. They secured these and then put the old people in charge of caring for them. This worked like a charm; soon there was spirited rivalry as to who could grow the best plant, the largest flowers.

They had found the old women dressed in somber dark clothes and by this time they knew that Trinidadians loved white and bright colors. They asked the stores for odd pieces of cloth and were sent quantities of bright colored prints. A group of ladies known as the Trinidadian Society came to the convent once a week and sat in the community room cutting out and sewing the long dresses with trains which the creole women loved.

It was a really exciting morning when, the clothing all ready to wear, the old women came into the chapel for prayers, each in her starched new dress, carrying the train gracefully over one arm, the fine embroidered petticoats showing under the skirts.

Sometimes, when they sat in the cool arcades where the sun's heat did not come directly, they told the sisters stories of earlier days in Trinidad, days when there were great sugar plantations, one next to the other. The planters and their families would come from the big houses to watch the dancing and throw handfuls of pennies among the dancers. In those days the English military bands in red coats played wonderful tunes, the old people said.

They had many anecdotes to tell too. "Once my aunt picked up an old stained silk purse on the beach, all white with salt water, and when she opened it there were old

Spanish gold coins in it," said one. Others would tell stories of long ago tragedies. There was the year 1854 when a ship from India brought the dreaded cholera to the island. People were taken sick and died a few hours later. All day and all night Archbishop Spaccapietra for whom the old peoples' home was named, would go about the city administering the Sacraments and giving people medicine from a chest he carried always with him.

"My mother said everybody loved him," said old Jessie. "Sometimes when a little baby was sick the doctor said he wouldn't live and the mother ran with it to the Archbishop to have him lay his hands on the baby and say a prayer over it. He used to smile but he never refused and my mother said the babies got well even when the doctor said they wouldn't. When the Archbishop left Trinidad the men took his horses out of his carriage and dragged it to the wharf themselves."

"And the people collected a big purse for him," chimed in another old woman, "but they didn't give it to him until he was on the ship. They knew if they did it sooner the purse would have been empty before the ship sailed."

There was another group of old ladies of a very different type at the Home. They lived in small cottages on the grounds and were called Les Pauvres Honteuses. These were aged ladies who had held good—a few very high—positions in the world but who now had no means at all and no relatives. A group of ladies of Port of Spain had furnished rooms in the hospice cottages for them and paid for their care. The old ladies were happy, for they had the independence needed to make them content. The dean of the group, so to speak, was the granddaughter of the French nobleman who had brought the first colonists

73

there and she kept an oil painting of her distinguished ancestor hung in her room.

The sisters had set up a little clinic. They had brought with them boxes of simple remedies and for several hours on certain mornings of the week people came crowding into the room, some with terrible sores which needed careful cleansing and dressing. Over each the sisters said a Hail Mary, no matter what the sufferer's faith.

Before long they found themselves called on to answer all sorts of demands. One Hindu woman came to ask "if you can christen me and marry me to my mister?" —a matter which they put in the hands of the nearby Dominican fathers. Another old Hindu came shaking her head and moaning, "plenty sick." She was given a dose of medicine and told to drink it, which she did obediently. Then, after thanking them, she explained further—"not me plenty sick. The Papa is." And one sweet faced old woman who said she had a bad pain, asked for a pill and added politely, "Any color at all, Sister."

One day a shaky old Mohammedan priest came in and explained that his daughter was being badly treated by her husband. Mohammed was being of no help at all in the matter and so he had come to ask the prayers of the sisters. "You can get nearer to God than I can," he explained.

The Archbishop wanted the sisters, in addition to their care of the old people, to open classes for fallen away Catholics as well as for those interested in the Faith. He wanted them to train his acolytes and hoped later they would undertake for him a census of children in the public schools and also of those not yet baptized.

The classes in religious instruction became very popular. Many came to them who had drifted from the Faith and needed only a helping hand to bring them back. There were only three in the class at first but by the end of the first year there were almost a hundred. Men came as well as women; usually after confirmation the men joined the local Holy Name Society and the women came together at the mothers' meetings.

The census the sisters had thought would be a minor task. They were given a map which they studied very carefully. It still looked simple, but it was a very different matter when they went to work. They had not realized how different was the reality from the flat map. The topography of Port of Spain consisted chiefly of hills.

"Is everything uphill?" groaned Sister Josephine, after days of climbing, sometimes a hundred steps to get to a house, sometimes a hill side with no steps at all. The little huts were so hidden in the hills that they were difficult to find even after one had climbed, but there were always eager little guides, willing, nay overwhelmingly insistent, on showing the sisters the way. Best of all was the welcome the census takers received. When they came to the last step or the last hill, there was always a glad cry of welcome when the black and white figures came in sight. It was equally a joy, the difficult climb achieved, to look out over the beauty spread out below them—the blue gulf with the little islands dotting it, the flat areas of orange groves, darkly green in the sun.

As with the old ladies at the Home, here too the experiences were often amusing as well as fruitful. Once

Sister Josephine succeeded in persuading one of the hill-top mothers to bring her twin babies to the church for baptism. She chose their names—Joseph and Dominic—and these met with maternal approval. Later, on another visit, she asked how Joseph and Dominic were getting along.

The mother looked puzzled. "No children with those names here," she said very positively. Sister Josephine asked her if she did not remember how she and the children's mother were both present when the babies had been given those names.

This cleared up the matter. "Oh, you mean George and William," she said, and let the puzzled Sister Josephine to a corner where, sleeping very peacefully in an orange crate, were the twins. Their mother explained the confusion: it was that the children were called by other names than those they received in baptism in case the devil came and asked for one of them.

"Then he say, 'I come for Joseph.' But here is only George, you see. So he go away, Sister, and he not get my boy."

The training of a band of acolytes proved an exciting task too. Each boy wanted to be the high acolyte, the one who rang the bell during Mass. There were heated arguments about this peaceful office, and these were settled by the sisters who had an uneasy fear that sometimes the boys did further settling of their own later. The old gardener came in sometimes to complain too, especially about a mango tree which always lost some of its fruit after the acolytes met for instructions.

When word spread about this class, mothers came to

ask if those of their children who were attending the public schools could perhaps come to the sisters to be prepared for their First Communion. The religious were happy to do this and in turn learned as they taught. For these children were very different from English children they had hitherto taught, much more mature and thoughtful. The answers they gave were sometimes unexpected too.

Once, when Sister Josephine asked her class why Jesus had chosen to be born in a poor stable instead of a fine house like the Governor's, there was no immediate answer. This the sisters had learned did not mean inattention or ignorance; it often meant the children were thinking over the question. Finally one small boy said, "Maybe He wanted a quiet life."

Of course there was the less thoughtful side of the picture too. One day, after a talk about the good Child at Bethlehem, who minded His parents so well, Sister was delighted to see how the lesson sunk in. The boys went out very quietly, as if under the spell of what they had just heard. She was still considering this with delight when a small boy of the class dashed in.

"Come, Sister, hurry. Philip and Mark dem fighting like two debbils."

Finally, after strenuous efforts on the part of both the educators and the educated, because of the loving labor of the sisters and the fact that the children were really anxious to make their First Communion, the great day was at hand. Little girls in flowing muslin skirts with veils right to the bottom of the skirts, little boys in stiff white suits and unaccustomed shoes marched to the convent chapel and went up like little angels to receive the

Lord. Then the march out again and the wonderful breakfast—chocolate and fresh rolls and little cakes. As final delight for the occasion there was a little bag of sweets for each to take home.

Trinidad was very proud of its hospital and its fine corps of doctors and staff of nurses. There the sisters went once a week on the day when the priests came to give Communion to the patients. Here too occurred the happy little human incidents. Once when Sister Josephine was going on her rounds, an old white-haired Indian called to her feebly. He had been baptized when he was a little boy, he told her, but ever since he had lived deep in the hills. Now he had been brought to the city and he knew he was going to die.

"You think God would like me so late as this?" he asked anxiously, and she assured him He would. A week later he made his First Communion and afterwards lay with his eyes closed, his hands still folded, a look of peace on his tired old face. That night he died.

One innovation carried out by the sisters was in regard to young girls who sometimes came to them, penniless, out of work, shelterless and frightened. Upstairs in the convent were four unused rooms and these were turned into dormitories. The sisters begged furniture from friends and kept the girls with them until they found work, and even then encouraged them to come back to tell them how they were getting along.

The year after they came to Trinidad the Archbishop asked them if they would visit the Carrera prison one afternoon a week and instruct any man who might wish this. It was a request which at first alarmed them, but they found the men so grateful for any attention that the weekly visit became a real joy. They took a little gulf steamer to reach the beautiful island on which the prison was situated, walked to the top of the hill and then to the chapel, where the men had made most of the fittings themselves. The candlesticks on the altar were made from old pieces of brass found in wreckage on the beach. The mural decorations and even the embroidery of the antependium had been made by the more aesthetic among the prisoners. Some of the work was crude, some very fine, but it was clear that it was all made with affection. And it was the work of men of many races and faiths—Catholic, Protestant, Chinese, Hindu, all proud of this little chapel whose interior was their own handiwork.

The sisters developed a regular program at Carrera. First, they all sang a hymn, preferably one with a fine marching rhythm and which the men could learn quickly. Then came an exposition of doctrine and after that the men were given the opportunity to ask any questions they wished. They had many to ask and it was always late in the afternoon before the sisters could leave. Boarding the steamer was not easy either. The pier was lower than the launch and the long habit and the scapular impeded them—"also the dear voluminous mantle plus an umbrella, plus sheets of music and catechism manuals," Sister Josephine wrote home ruefully.

Perhaps only the hospital work was as rewarding as this work among the prisoners. To see men return to the Sacraments after twenty years and more away from them was enough to take away weariness and occasional discouragement. The sisters said that if the patients and the prisoners gained a great deal, so did they who came among them. They felt a deepening sense of the mercy and the love of God, an increase in faith, a greater realization of the need and the efficacy of prayer.

## SEVEN

WHEN THE WAR ENDED CORPUS CHRISTI HOUSE IN LON-
don was closed. The sisters returned to Leicester. Some of
them were not to be there for long, however, for the community was making ready to open another foreign mission.

Soon after the first mission had been opened in Trinidad, the Corpus Christi Sisters accepted another, this
time in faraway America, where Bishop McNicholas had
asked them to staff a house which he promised to secure
for them and where he hoped to carry out the variety of
works which his fellow Dominicans in England had told
him these sisters were engaged in there.

Some years before, Father McNabb had visited the
United States and stayed with the Dominican Fathers at

St. Vincent Ferrer parish in New York. There he had spoken to a certain Father John about the sisters working with him in his Leicester parish. Now, named bishop of a vast northwestern diocese, he remembered Father McNabb's sisters and wrote to ask if they would make a foundation there. He listed as incentives to their coming the scattered Catholic families, the few schools, the children with no religious instruction. No doubt he knew that missionary zeal loves to have the difficulties listed.

Prudence of course told Sister Mary to refuse him. The members were still few in number and Trinidad had further depleted them. Besides, as that work increased, even more would be needed. They were so poor that the journey would prove prohibitive. But before Sister Mary could offer this as a valid excuse, Miss Bjerring of New York, a Catholic teacher whom Father McNabb had met while he was in the United States, offered to pay their fares and also their maintenance for some months. So the community voted to take up the work.

"Now you are everywhere the merest sprinkling," wrote Father McNabb from Hawksyard Priory, but it was clear he wrote jubilantly rather than fearfully to his "little family of my sisters in Saint Dominic who are going across the ocean for the care of souls." They were setting out like discoverers, into an uncertainty. They were taking God on trust. He was writing this letter to them on the feast day of one of their elder sisters—Catherine of Siena, who had gone across the sea, too, even though it was only from Genoa to Marseilles, a girl in her teens and unafraid. "God speed you and love you and fill your hands with sheaves," the letter ended.

They put it away carefully. Even when Father McNabb wrote prose, it sounded like poetry.

For this mission Sister Mary had decided to go with her sisters and see them settled. It had been found very difficult to secure a ship for everyone was going to the States. The boats were filled with soldiers and war workers, as well as with many who were going to make a home in the New World. Eventually three places were secured and Sister Mary, Sister Mercedes and Sister Teresa sailed on the *Philadelphia* on May first. With them went three children who were returning to the United States, having been unable to do so while the war was still going on. These they were to pick up in London at a house in which they had been invited to spend the night.

It was an orphanage, a big ugly building with a long line of dormitories. It was in the charge of an elderly woman known only as Miss Kate and she cared there for the destitute little children brought to her. Sister Mary had heard about her from both Father Herbert Thurston and the writer Enid Dennis, but this was the first time she had met her.

In the evening, when the children were in bed, she came to talk with the religious. She had wanted to be a religious herself, she told them. It was now almost fifty years ago that she had entered Carmel as an out sister, but after a few months it was clear she had not the health for that rigorous life. She tried once more, this time with a community in France, but again her health made it impossible for her to stay. Her confessor of years, a Carmelite, brought her to St. Mary's Home, for he knew she loved children and that children were devoted to her. But she had not really wanted to stay there.

"It was when I saw the dirt and disorder in the house and the sad condition of the little children when they first came there that I thought this was what God wanted of me. And I had had a dream of Our Lord and of Our Blessed Lady and what they said to me made me feel this was to be my work."

It had not been easy. Miss Fanny, the woman in charge, was old and not too good a manager. Many of the sixty and more children were little more than babies. She had voluntary helpers and they were not always reliable. But she stayed with Miss Fanny until the latter died. She was quick with the needle and she and her helpers made albs and altar cloths—"and even some trousseaux" she said smilingly—and so earned money for the always impoverished house. Miss Fanny had died twenty years before and since that time Miss Kate had been in full charge.

"I love it all," she told Sister Mary. "There is only one thing I wish I could find time for now and then—a retreat. But I couldn't leave the children that long. In fact," she said, "it is a real and a rare treat for me to hear a sermon."

Even during the brief time they were at the Home, the sisters saw how clean and well fed were her little charges. She was poor, that was evident, but it was also evident that she was not poor in love. Though the clothing of her little charges was old and plain, it was clean and well mended too.

Before they left England the three sisters wanted to make their confessions. They went to a nearby church where the priest knew nothing whatsoever of the work

*Mother Mary of the Blessed Sacrament,*
*1919*

It was to me as if I were walking in glory to think I had carried out the Lord's command, and that His majesty had taken me, who am so poor and mean, for His instrument in so great a work. So happy was I, that I felt as if I were lifted up out of my very self.

*Facsimile of Mother Mary's handwriting*
*found in one of her books after her death*
*—a quotation of St. Teresa of Avila.*

Sister Mary was embarking on, nor did she tell him. But he kept her for a few minutes after the absolution to impress on her the confidence she must have in God and devotion to His mother. Not until she was on the ship did Sister Mary remember that Our Lady was the patroness of America and realize what a coincidence it was that the strange priest spoke to her thus on the very eve of her going to that country.

The voyage was uneventful. The sisters delivered the children to their parents and then went to the convent of the Dominican Sisters of the Sick Poor on East 69th Street. There they met a woman who in some ways reminded them of Sister Kate.

Mary Walsh had come to the United States from Ireland; the one thing she could do was housework, but the thing she wanted most to do was to work for the Lord and especially for His poor. She met a Dominican priest to whom she confided her hope and he told her of certain people in the neighborhood who were too poor to procure care in their home. She took care of them as best she could. Later a few others joined her in the work. Now they had become Dominicans, a group who were devoting their lives to the sick poor, taking care of them in their own homes. It was evident that here was another group who served the Lord with gladness. The sisters were so gay and cheerful one would think their days were filled with pleasant work instead of tasks thankless, tiring and completely hidden in God.

During the several days they spent with Mother Mary Walsh, she and Sister Mary Ellerker had long talks together. Mother Mary knew how young in her work was the other religious; she knew that she had days of difficulty and anxiety before her and she tried to give her courage. One evening she took the younger woman's hands in her own workworn ones and said, in a very humble way, that perhaps her own experience would be of a little help. There might be opposition to what she wanted to do, she warned Sister Mary, and sometimes it would come from very good people, even from those of their faith. She spoke of the founding of her own community, of the misunderstanding as to what they planned to do, the hardships in the way of finding money and houses—but the much greater difficulty from those in the Church who did not want such work started at all. Mother Mary made it clear, however, that there were always to be found some who stood by you, who understood that it was a matter of souls as well as of caring for bodies.

"Eventually you will find that everything else is small in comparison," said Mother Mary earnestly, "that nothing matters except souls."

To the convent came Miss Bjerring, who had guaranteed the cost of their coming and who took them about New York. Her own history, they found, had been an interesting one. Her father had been an Orthodox priest who later became a Catholic layman. Bering Straits had been named for one of his ancestors who was among the first to come to America; with time the name had been altered, but the family preserved the original spelling. The daughter was herself a Dominican tertiary and felt she had a definite vocation to a religious life.

She showed the sisters places of interest—the Metropolitan Museum, St. Patrick's Cathedral, and Central Park in the course of a long drive. They dined with her and were served an entirely American dinner, beginning with blue fish and ending with ice cream. They told their hostess that already they were learning the language of the new land. "Sweets" for instance were called by the odd name of candy; a tram was a street car; a draper's shop was a dry goods store.

The three travelers said goodbye to Mother Mary and her sisters and to Miss Bjerring who went with them to the train. They soon found out that trains were different in the New World, too, and also in the services they offered. Scarcely were they seated when a colored woman came up and offered them three big empty bags.

"But what are we to do with them?" asked Sister Mary.

The woman looked at their veils. "They'll keep the dust off your bonnets, lady. They come in mighty handy." So they accepted the bags but did not use them, thinking it something of a joke. In the morning they were less sure, for everything, including their veils, was covered with a fine thick layer of coal dust.

They had not changed the time of their watches as they went farther west, planning to do it when they arrived. While they waited to change trains in Chicago, in a station which looked more like a church than a railroad depot, they heard a man intoning at intervals. It sounded as if a religious service were being conducted near at hand. Then a man appeared and they heard what he was saying so melodiously: he was announcing the time the trains left!

During the next few days they often wondered, as they looked from their windows, why Americans went to Europe to look at scenery when they had this magnificence of their own. Museums and palaces and cathedrals—artistic treasures of the ages—to come to see these was understandable. But nearly all the Americans they had met in England had come to see the mountains or the lakes. They never said a word about the magnificence of their own country.

One thing the sisters found very hard to meet at first: the unaffected cordiality and frank curiosity people showed towards them. They had the British passion for privacy but it was clear these Americans did not have it and did not even notice others did. On the trains people came up to them, visited with them for a while and asked all manner of questions—who they were, where they were going, where they came from and what they were going to do. In fact, there were some who asked why they were doing it!

They went continuously west in their journey and then began to climb north. The land grew wilder and quantities of slim swaying birch trees and many lakes appeared. It was easy, when one remembered stories read in childhood, to realize that Indians had lived there, that, in fact, there were still some in many of these areas.

At last they reached Duluth, their destination. On the platform stood two people who introduced themselves as Dr. Magie and his wife and who took them to a car. "Just get right in," said the Doctor encouragingly. "Don't you people feel a bit nervous. We're glad you're here and we'll take good care of you, ladies."

At first sight Duluth seemed all hills and lakes, with no level streets at all and all the houses set on hill tops. However, they were given little time to see the city for their hosts told them they had arrived just in time for

Mass and took them to the cathedral. It was in every sense a Mass of thanksgiving—for their safe coming, for the pleasant journey, for the kind reception and for the place to which God had brought them. They felt at home and happy.

After Mass the Magies took them home for breakfast and then drove them to their new home, high on one of the hills, 600 feet above Lake Superior. As they drove up to the door they were delighted to see that the name of the house was already over the door. In large letters the inscription read: Corpus Christi House. On the steps of the porch stood waiting to welcome them Mrs. Wall, head of the group known in the city as Hilltop Workers, who had made the house ready for them. It was pleasantly warmed, too, for though it was May the weather was still cold in Duluth and the central heat was welcome. But they smiled to think they were to sleep in heated cells.

"That is something only the sick have in England," Sister Mary explained. "In fact, a fire in an English bedroom all but supposes that the one sleeping there is ill."

Mrs. Wall smiled. "The winters are bitter cold here, and you will find fires in your bedroom not a luxury but a real necessity—even in May."

After the kindly neighbors had gone, the sisters went over their new property and all but got lost in the house which was very large. The chapel was most attractive, with its wooden altar with hand carved symbols, and with three large windows. The stations of the cross were very unusual, being photographs in round hand carved frames. In the sacristy was a large vestment chest. That very evening Sister Mary named Sister Teresa sacristan, much to the latter's delight.

They went from this pleasant chapel back to the very pleasant living room and the clean kitchen and found there an incredible amount of food—cakes, rolls, doughnuts, preserves, meat, butter, milk, eggs.

That evening three very thankful people went to the chapel to say the Office. There might be hard work ahead but it was clear that they had come to a pleasant place. The ordo of the day directed that the Office of Saint Andrew be recited and this they did. And a little later a lovely thing happened.

In New York Miss Bjerring had told Sister Mary she had something which she wished to give the new foundation, something she treasured very much. In fact, it had been given to her by the bishop to whose diocese they were going. There had been no time to look at the contents of the little package before they left. It had been carefully wrapped and Sister Mary had placed it in the sack with the sacred vessels, for she realized it was a relic. After they had finished the Office, Sister Teresa went to bring the little gift and open it. To their delight it was a relic of Blessed Andrew, whose office they had just said. It would have, they decided, a place close to the altar in their chapel.

Next day the Bishop came to see them, a still youthful man, clad in the familiar Dominican garb. He had not been able to come to meet them at the train for he had had a confirmation ceremony but he had come as soon as he could to make them welcome. He asked about Father McNabb whom he knew and the congregation in England. He went through the house with them and saw they had been well taken care of. Before he left he blessed them and promised that next morning they would hear

Mass in their own chapel. He would send them a priest.

Not until they were ready to go to bed did they discover that the house which had seemed so completely furnished did lack one important item: a bell. "Until we get one let's not lose each other in this big place," said Sister Mercedes.

In the morning, to their joy, it was the Bishop himself who came to say Mass. Afterwards he reserved the Blessed Sacrament there. Sister Mary's emotion was deep when she learned they were to have the Lord in their house. It was the first time the sisters, who had just come from England, had that longed-for privilege which Father McNabb had said was so necessary but which had never been allowed them there. They were to have Mass daily in the house, the Bishop told them; Father McCarthy would come to say it.

The Bishop was still at the house when some of the Hilltop Workers arrived. He thanked all who had worked so hard to make the new home attractive. It delighted the newcomers to hear him, for they felt he was saying exactly what they wanted to say but much better than they could phrase it.

During their first week they went about Duluth, visiting the houses in their area in the hope of finding some Catholics who would be glad to hear that Our Lord was now close to them. But when Sister Mercedes and Sister Teresa came together after several hours to give the results of their search, it was to learn that between them they had located exactly one Catholic family!

To make up for that depressing beginning several Benedictine sisters came to see them. Mother Chrysostom, the Mother General, gave the newcomers an affectionate welcome and said they were to call on her for anything they needed or wanted to know. Bishop McNicholas had already told them about these sisters who had been in the area since early pioneer days.

"The Duluth diocese owes to them a large part of its Catholicity," he said. "What Catholic schools there are were opened by them. Theirs was the first Catholic academy here and they have a college, a hospital, an orphanage and a home for the aged."

Other people came to call and offer help—Madame Poirier, one of Duluth's first settlers, and her daughter who was an expert in social work; Mrs. Haley in whose home the sisters were to hold catechism classes and who promised to send them a check each month.

Only one disappointment came to pass during their first weeks in the new home. On Sunday they went to the Cathedral to Mass and waited to hear the announcements about the feast of Corpus Christi, especially the time of the procession and what else was planned to honor the Blessed Sacrament on that day. But the announcements ended with not a word spoken about Corpus Christi except mention of the Mass for that day. They looked at each other in dismay, realizing there would be no procession, no celebration of their beloved day.

Later the three discussed having a procession by themselves, but that seemed rather ridiculous. Three people simply did not make a procession. Reluctantly they let the day go by unsung and uncelebrated. But the next year, when they had children under instruction, they promised each other it would be very different.

One of the first things which Bishop McNicholas asked them to do was to take charge of the Sunday school attached to St. Peter's Church. This was an Italian parish and the sisters there were to meet with a variety of children who were, as Sister Teresa wrote home, "restless, tiresome and affectionate, whose attention wanders until you are figuratively ready to slay them—and then look at you with such innocent laughing eyes that your wrath is instantly disarmed."

One hot July day the sisters brought the children to Corpus Christi House for a picnic. Everyone was warm and bedraggled from playing games and running races and sticky from candy and fruit. The sisters felt as hot and mussed as their charges, when suddenly Sister Mercedes came up to announce in a tragic whisper, "Two Bishops!"

There stood Bishop McNicholas and with him another whom he introduced as Bishop McVevitt of Harrisburg, smilingly enjoying the party, much the worse for happy wear. The sisters felt hotter and stickier than ever, but their young guests were not a whit troubled. They smiled their usual confiding smiles and the dignified visitors smiled back.

Since there seemed little chance for a parochial school in the near future, the sisters had promised to conduct catechism classes with St. Peter's as the center. Each day from three to five they went to the church and the children came to them direct from the public school. They came very regularly too, somewhat to the surprise of the sisters, and proved a very attentive group.

The religious also began parish visiting in the mornings, preparing the sick for the Sacraments, and trying to get the grown ups to come regularly to Mass. They opened Americanization classes among the Italian women, working with the Americanization group in the city.

They had been badly in need of some instrument on which they could play while the children sang. Apparently someone had heard of this, for one day a wagon drove up and in it was an organ, a gift for the house.

"Come here quickly," called Sister Mary, and Sister Teresa, who was washing dishes, ran out still carrying a tea towel. She stared in pure happiness at the organ. It was the second gift brought to the house that morning.

"Two things I have been longing for," she said. "Music and a dog. Now we have both."

Bishop McNicholas had told Sister Mary that one way in which they might augment their income was by the baking of altar breads. The Benedictine sisters had done this but were now so busy that they would be happy to relinquish it into other hands. When Sister Mary agreed to try it, he said he would bring the electric plate on which the breads were made.

He brought the plate but he did more than that: he gave the sisters their first lesson in baking altar breads. With a very serious look on his face, he mixed the batter and then showed the sisters how to pour the batter on the plate.

"I learned this in my student days in the novitiate," he said, as he stood contemplating with pride his very fine results, "and I became very expert. Now watch me carefully once more and then I am sure you can do it by yourselves."

This work, begun under such auspicious episcopal direction, was later continued in other houses of the congregation until eventually the sisters were making a great many. Thousands of breads were sent out weekly to churches throughout the diocese.

On the feast of Our Lady of Mount Carmel the sisters had a visitor, a priest from the east whom they had been anxious to meet—Father Clement Thuente, a close friend of the Bjerring family, and for many years prior of the Church of St. Vincent Ferrer in New York City.

Father Thuente told them stories of his years in that parish and the converts of those days—Rose Hawthorne Lathrop who had founded a Dominican congregation to care for the cancerous poor; Mrs. Annie Arnold, a devoted tertiary, whose husband had been head of a great department store in the city and who had set up the first Catholic settlement house, next to the Church of St. Rose of Lima; Marian Gurney, who came to help her and later became the foundress of the congregation of the Sisters of Christian Doctrine.

The sisters to whom he was speaking, all of them converts, greatly enjoyed this information and in turn told Father Thuente of the converts who worked with them at Leicester—Emily Fortey and Anne McDiarmid and the two who called themselves Michael Field—all of them Dominican tertiaries.

One day their chaplain, Father Patrick O'Riordan, invited them to visit with him a parishioner at a settlement called Cohasset. He thought they might find a vocation there. When Sister Mary asked if it were far, he said vaguely, "Just a short train journey."

This proved to be something of an understatement. But it was a wonderfully exciting trip and the sisters wrote home about it later, waxing poetic over the beauty they had seen.

"We have dipped our hands in the waters of the Mississippi," ran one letter. "We have walked through the dense woods of the northwest. We have listened to the strange cry of the American rook and watched the flying flame of the redwing. With noble pines on either hand, with stars above us and white sand at our feet, the faint tinkle of bells and the croaking of the frogs only making the silence and peace deeper, we have stood on a broad bridge over the Father of Waters and watched the light playing on the surface of the water."

It was unusually fervent language for the restrained English, but there was little doubt that they were greatly moved by the sight, and again they wondered why Americans went to Europe for scenery.

Much of this sightseeing was due to miscalculations of Father O'Riordan: the train they had intended to take no longer ran, for the schedule had been changed some weeks before. They started later in the day and at first the route took them through blackened forests where a terrible forest fire had raged the year before. It was a relief to come to lakes and green trees again. They left the train for the bus at a stop called Grand Rapids and there they saw for the first time the popular American concoction known as Cracker Jack. Fascinatedly they watched three small boys gnawing their way through the contents of the boxes, at the same time carpeting the floor of the bus with brown and white fragments.

A car took them the last ten miles of their journey—

the short train trip which had already taken most of the day. They drove down a long brown road with the great river at their left, straight into a wonderful sunset with all colors from palest blue to gold and purple.

"How glad I am we missed that train," whispered Sister Mercedes, and Sister Mary said she had just been saying over to herself the words from the morning Office: "The heavens declare the glory of the Lord."

Fortunately at the end of the trip they found pleasant people who were very willing to put them all up for the night. In the morning they went to Mass in a tiny chapel, with only six others present as congregation, but they were fervent. There was also a small altar boy who had to be assisted now and then with the responses and who quite forgot to say the Confiteor at all.

The vocation failed to show up but, back in their house in Duluth, the sisters agreed it had been a wonderful journey.

On December 10, Mother Mary—a short time before, Bishop McNicholas had insisted she be called by that title now since she headed three foundations in three lands—left for a visitation of England and Trinidad. It would be her first visit to the latter foundation.

Since it was clear that more vocations would be needed, and quickly, if the sisters were to do what they hoped in the United States, Bishop McNicholas had arranged for Mother Mary a visit to Ireland before going to Trinidad, to seek vocations there. He promised to pay her own fare and that of any possible new members.

It proved a very successful mission, for she sent on three girls and had the promise of six others who came not long afterwards. Trinidad was a fascinating place, she wrote, and she would have much to tell the Duluth sisters on her return.

"I shall bring you a very interesting visitor today," Father O'Riordan told the sisters one day after Mass. "I am going to introduce you to one of the real pioneers."

By this time the sisters knew that their work in America was to be definitely a missionary task. They knew that their bishop had in his diocese many localities without church or priest or religious to carry on the catechetical work at centers. He had eight mission chapels that had no resident priest and at least sixty mission stations which had not even a small chapel. Later when the sisters went to some of these isolated places on missions, staying a month or six weeks in each, they came home sad because so little could be accomplished in so limited a time. To stay a whole year at one mission—but that was only a dream. Even so, the sisters were assured that the situation was much better than it had been a few years before.

The visitor whom Father O'Riordan brought had been a missionary during those early difficult days. Monsignor Buh was very old, with a long white beard. His tall form was stooped with the weight of his almost ninety years. But his blue eyes were still eager and his voice had a fine timbre.

The young Irish sisters sat around him on the floor and listened wide-eyed to his stories of long ago, of Indians, of the wild wastes over which the priests journeyed to go to isolated little groups, to whom they could come at best only once a year.

"An archdiocese and several dioceses cover now the territory where I first worked," he said. "The weather was the hardest thing of all to fight—the cold and the storms and the bitter winds." He looked so frail as he sat there that it seemed impossible to think that he had once been a strong young man and able to battle the elements.

Up to that time the sisters had heard only the more ordinary stories of this northeast. Priests who had been in the United States and priests around Duluth spoke of early days, too, but this old man reached farther into the past. He spoke of buffalo hunts, of the wily Sioux, of winning souls in a primitive land where the Chippewas owned what was now Wisconsin and the Sioux were lords of the Dakotas.

"Well," said Sister Mercedes thoughtfully, after Monsignor Buh had gone, "if you want to draw any conclusions from his life I think the rule would be: live in the open air and sleep there too sometimes. Have the plainest food and not much of it. Think only of souls and never of yourself. You will then be healthy and happy and live a long time."

They learned his life story from Bishop McNicholas. He was born in Laichingen in 1833, an ancient city which in his day was under Hapsburg rule. After his ordination he served for six years in his own diocese, then answered an appeal from the New World. He came to Minnesota when Duluth was a trading post for Indians and the few white men there. For a time he was very busy studying the Chippewa language, which he learned thoroughly. The first retreat he attended consisted of Bishop Grace and 29 priests, which was the entire number then caring for all of Minnesota, the two Dakotas and part of Wisconsin. He founded little churches in various outposts, for the Poles and the Canadians and the Irish. He served where he was needed and the need was great.

He was later honored for his work, too, for Leo XIII made him a domestic prelate, and he was also named first vicar of Duluth, a title which he still held. He was living the evening of his life with a group of young priests in a house which bore his name—the Buh Mission House.

"He never holds us back," one priest said earnestly to the sisters. "Sometimes we feel he is no older than we are, he is so eager and so interested and so willing to work."

The sisters had heard so much about Indians that they hoped some day to do work among them, too, but this they hardly expected since it was not in the line of duties set for them. In fact, the first Indians they saw were three who got lost on their way to the Benedictine convent and came to their door to ask the way. They were tall men, dark faced and solemn. But they were curious, too, and wanted to know where these new religious came from. The sisters told them from across the sea, from England, but they were now going to live in Duluth.

"Are you Americans?" asked one of the Irish sisters innocently.

The oldest Indian drew himself up even straighter. "We are the only Americans," he said briefly.

During the summer, the sisters were invited to come to Superior to meet the famous photographer of the Indians, D.F. Barry, a great friend of the Sioux. He had not only a large collection of pictures which he had taken but also many mementos which they had given him. He showed the sisters some of these—the scalping knife of one chief, the hunting shirt of another. The sisters looked at these articles with interest but they turned with much greater pleasure to the lovely little beaded hood made for a papoose princess of the tribe.

It would have taken several days to look at all the display, and the pictures would have taken a week. Mr. Barry selected a few of his favorites from among the latter. "Here are two of the greatest chiefs among them all," he said. "These are Chief Gallo and Chief Joseph—both very devout Catholics."

He showed them his own favorite among all the chiefs—Thunder Hawk, who had been the devoted friend of Father DeSmet and who had more than once come secretly and in haste to warn the black robe that hostile Indians were planning to kill him. Once he told him he must find someone to protect him on his journey. The "someone" was Mrs. Galpin, the trader's wife, who offered to ride her horse close beside the priest. The Indians lying in wait did not dare shoot, lest they hit her.

"The old chief is dead now," said Mrs. Barry. "I wish the Catholics would put up a stone to mark the place in South Dakota where he is buried."

There were pictures of many more chiefs, some with very picturesque names—Rain-in-the-Face and Sitting Bull among them. There was also a picture of Sitting Bull's little daughter who bore the odd but lovely name of Standing Holy. This picture their host gave them as a gift.

The sisters from the Old World learned many things about the New World during their first year there. For one thing they now knew the amazing number of nationalities represented in Duluth—twenty-eight. And already they were involved in work they had not expected to be called on to do: a little Polish girl of ten who was the subject of litigation between her own mother and a foster mother was given to them to take care of, pending a legal decision.

They had learned not only new customs during that first year but also a new climate. They had not known there could be so much snow as in their corner of Minnesota. They learned that 25 or even 35 degrees below zero was not unusual and that it was hard work to make a path from their door to the street and to keep the furnace high enough to keep the house warm enough so that the pipes, as well as themselves, did not freeze.

Sister Teresa made the snow sweeping a little easier by singing as she worked a little song she had written about it. The first two lines ran:

*"Oh, give me a shovel and give me a broom,*
*And I'll sweep the snow from your living room."*

# EIGHT

Mother Mary, after an absence of six months, returned to her foundation in Duluth in June of 1921. The house in England was getting along very well, she reported, and all was well in Trinidad.

Though she came back to the United States with interesting accounts of both houses, it was in Trinidad that the more dramatic things happened. Climate, conditions and the people all contributed to produce a life very different from that of England.

She had many stories to tell of their tropical foundation, including the touching one of a young woman, a patient at the hospital to which the sisters came each week. The girl was in a very disturbed condition, and when Sister Josephine came into the ward she was screaming in delirium and the other patients were restless and some were weeping in sympathy. The card at the foot of the bed listed her as a Catholic.

Sister Josephine went very close to the patient and stooped over her. The girl was utterly unaware of her as she made the sign of the Cross over her, and then, very distinctly and close to her ear, spoke the act of contrition. The eyes remained closed, the face was still contorted as if with pain, but gradually the screaming grew fainter and finally stopped entirely. In a few minutes she was sleeping quietly.

"It was almost," said Mother Mary, "as if the words of the prayer she knew had penetrated to the poor troubled brain and brought her relief."

Her Duluth group told Mother Mary of the work there while she was away, especially that among the Indians. The Bishop, troubled because so little was being done for them in his diocese, little materially and even less spiritually, had worked out a plan and put it into action by going himself to the first station when it was opened. This worked so well that he went to others and found how few of the people had ever seen a bishop. At Grand Portage, once an important fur trading center and now an Indian reservation, he learned that this was the first time in thirty-two years that a bishop had come there.

To help the Corpus Christi Sisters teach the children their catechism at these stations, he had selected two women who could speak both English and Chippewa. The work had not proved difficult, for the Indian children were very good and very willing to learn. A much greater difficulty was finding accommodations for the sisters who had to spend the night sometimes in very primitive places.

Usually one of the families found room for them and occasionally they slept in tents.

They told Mother Mary stories of a month spent on one Chippewa reservation, very poor and neglected. The chief came out to greet them in person, pleasantly and affably. He spoke only in Chippewa, however, and no one at the reservation spoke English either. The instructions had to wait until an interpreter was secured.

It was very cold when they came there and in order to get water from the rain barrel a thick coating of ice had to be chopped off with a hatchet. This reservation had a tiny chapel and one day a priest came to say Mass and administer the Sacraments. The water for Mass froze before it could be used and had to be melted.

They told her that their days on this reservation made them feel they were actually living through the pioneer experiences which Monsignor Buh had told them about. It was not only a matter of cold either; it was the people among whom they worked. One morning they had gone to call on a woman. They knocked at the door and it was opened with great violence, disclosing a woman holding a huge knife high in the air. She let it fall, much to her visitors' relief, when she saw who they were. She explained in broken English that only half breeds knocked at the door; she was always armed when she answered a knock. In the next house the sisters found a seventeen-year-old Indian girl, married three years before and deserted by her husband. She proved a good girl and eager to work, and the sisters decided to take her back with them to Duluth.

During that month they had learned that it was not very difficult to get Indians to come to services. It was, however, very hard to get them to go home afterwards. They stayed for hours and left only when they were put out.

Once Sister Immaculata, who had learned, as she thought, the Chippewa word for bishop, was using it with confidence, when she noticed some of her listeners were smiling. She learned later that she had left out one syllable of the word and was calling Bishop McNicholas Big Bear.

"But the most interesting thing I learned about the Chippewa tongue," she told Mother Mary, "is that in that language there is no word of cursing, no oath. If an Indian wants to swear he has to do it in the white man's language."

Sometimes at night when they looked from their cabin they saw the northern lights, wonderful swiftly moving fountains of light and color. And even as they were flashing over the horizon, the sky was still blue in the west and a few early stars hung low.

They assured her that though it had been hard work they had enjoyed their month on the mission. And before they left for home, when the visiting priest came there, he was a delighted man. "The wonderful sisters corralled twenty for baptism," he had reported in Duluth.

This was the beginning of the mission visiting which was to form a part of their lives for the next years. All the work they carried out in Duluth certainly paled beside it in surprises, hardships and fine results.

A somewhat similar work was the summer vacation schools. The sisters would live in a small town for from two to five weeks; sometimes it was not really a town at all or even a real settlement, but merely a group of isolated houses in the country. Water was always scarce; a cup of the precious fluid was often one's allowance for a whole day of washing hands and faces. Often the sisters walked for miles over hot and dusty roads during the summer, which was as hot as the winter was cold. The food was poor and often scanty, but it was the best there was and it was offered generously. They slept in an Indian hut or a crowded little house. Sometimes there was what was called a hotel, where the furniture consisted of a bed and a box, but even so these rooms were treasured by the sisters, for they had both a door and a key. The huts had only open spaces for a door and the sisters used a sheet or blanket hung up to give them a little privacy.

However, the greatest hardship of those summers was the lack of water. In seasons of drought it was all but non-existent, and Sister Teresa said she envied the house cat which was perfectly happy with its own method of washing.

The school season of vacation lasted from May to October, the period of the long vacation. Often in the places where the sisters stayed there was no chapel; sometimes there was a poor little building, closed for most of the time. During their missions a priest sometimes came to stay and then the missionaries knew their greatest possible joy, for during his time there the Blessed Sacrament was reserved.

"How spoiled are we who have always lived near a fine church with everything in it as it should be," said Sister Mercedes thoughtfully one day, thinking of Leicester and London. "How wonderful it is to see Our Lord here before these poor people whose struggle to make a living is so unending and so hard. They need Him so and it is so wonderful when they have Him."

Sometimes the teaching was close enough to Duluth so that they could come home each day, but the same poverty was there, too. Once Sister Teresa and Sister Mercedes went to a new mission stop, Markville. There a priest and a small group of people were waiting. It did not take long to see all of Markville—a few shacks, a tiny store, a little white Protestant chapel and a disused schoolhouse which served as the Catholic Church. Inside were a few benches, a plain altar, a statue of Our Lady and a tiny organ.

There were also some twenty candidates for catechism study, ranging in age from four to seventeen, ready and waiting. Sister Teresa took those who had already made their First Communion and Sister Mercedes took the rest, including the tall gangling youth who said he felt it was time for him to make his First Communion. Two of the younger of the candidates were later discovered to be the four and six year old sons of the Methodist minister. They had simply wandered into the party. Sister Mercedes had given the younger a small holy picture which he vociferously refused to give up. He ran out with it clutched in his hand and Sister Mercedes devoutly hoped that his father would not be too shocked.

The lesson ended with the reciting of the rosary which most of them knew and, before they left the town, Sister Mercedes took a snapshot of them all standing on the steps of the little school. They had been invited to tea in one of the little homes and were given the hospitality which, said Sister Teresa, seems the inheritance of the very poor the world over. Then they were presented with a big bunch of wild flowers and took the train for Duluth. It had been a very successful day.

There were so many unbaptized children in isolated areas that the Sisters worked hard to make possible the conferring of at least this Sacrament. The time and the place were arranged, a priest promised to come, and the ceremony took place. But of course it was not always as simple as that. Once in a small town of Polish settlers nine children, ranging in age from three months to nine years, were to be baptized in the little church on a Saturday afternoon.

On Friday evening the priest who had a mission in the town received word that he must leave very early Saturday for another town. If the children were to be baptized it must be between then and early on Saturday. Two kind people were found who had autos and who agreed to take the children there and bring them home again. However, the cars did not reach all the homes until almost nine that night and some of the parents could with difficulty be persuaded to take the children from their beds and let them go out into the dark night. Some were taken in their night clothes, wrapped in blankets, and sound asleep. By ten o'clock the little church was reached. There were no lights except the sanctuary lamp until two altar candles were lighted.

The children were all awake now and they were ranged along the altar rail, the heads of some barely reaching it. One sister held a flashlight to help the priest read the ritual and another held the three months baby, and, with him in her arms, went up and down the line, sponsoring for them all.

The incident had a beauty of its own—the little

shadowy church, the dim sanctuary where the candles shone upon the tabernacle door, the row of small heads, the anxious godfather who was the driver of one of the cars, the absorbed face of the young priest. As soon as it was over they all drove back. It was after midnight before the last child was in his own home and in bed again.

It was in that same area, on a later mission, that the sisters found a large family of children whose mother shook her head when she was asked if they were baptized. "Are you Catholics?" she was asked and began to shake her head again. Then suddenly she burst into tears and ran into the house. She came back with a Catholic certificate of marriage and showed it to them.

The sisters made arrangements for a mass baptism for the next day and promised transportation for her and the children. When they came they found the children and their mother waiting, their arms full of roses, so many that it was clear that she had stripped her garden. She explained that she had heard that during the mission the Blessed Sacrament was reserved; the roses were for the altar.

It was the children they taught who gave the hard working sisters their greatest reward. They were so eager for instruction that often they walked long distances to come. They would long remember two Polish girls of ten and twelve who walked four times a week while they were being prepared for First Communion—twelve miles to the church and twelve miles home again, always smiling and cheerful despite the hot sun and the rough roads. When the mission sisters felt almost too tired to go on, the thought of the little Polish girls, their blue eyes bright under the flaxen braids, who never once failed to come to the class, gave them fresh courage for their work.

Mother Mary who, once back from her visitation, had remained for some time in the States, said one day that she found it always a joy to listen to people talk about the mission fields in which they worked, but it sometimes astonished her how it seemed to be taken for granted that all souls needing mission help lived in China or Africa or India.

"It is not that I am not happy to know that these generous missionaries receive help and a great deal of it," she said. "It is only that sometimes one can't help wondering whether people realize that a great deal of help is also needed for the mission fields at home."

But she was very grateful to the understanding ones who did bring help, and there were many about Duluth, among them the convert who gave unlimited use of his car; and himself gathered children from scattered farms and brought them to one place for instruction.

Sometimes too the people were able to help themselves if only one helped them with suggestions. In one little fishing village Mass was said once a month in the school house, but the people wanted a real church and they got one by the simple expedient of providing it themselves. They found a small unused shack. They gave all the time they could spare from their days full of hard work to replastering it and mending the floors and giving it a coat of paint. It was a wonderful day for them all when a visiting priest offered Mass in the very small but very authentic church.

One day a new and different work came to the sisters.

A social worker in Duluth came to their house to tell them about a young girl in difficulties who needed a place to stay. The only place the social worker had been able to think of in this emergency was the Corpus Christi group, and so she came to them to ask help.

Mother Mary agreed without delay. This proved to be the beginning of a work which was to grow greatly in the years which followed. When, twenty years later, they counted up the number of girls who had been with them during that time it amounted to almost two thousand. Many of them were girls coming from the country, often guileless and innocent and led astray rather than deliberately seeking the wrong path. Those who watched this work and its success said it stemmed from two things: the sisters had a religious base to offer the girls and also considered each as an individual, a member of the family, and a part of the home where she was staying. They planned always individual mothering, as much freedom as possible, and also instruction in household work as well as baby care for the unmarried mothers among them.

There were of course some with whom they failed, but by far the greater majority of their girls could be called successes. The letters they sent to Corpus Christi House after they left there showed that. They came from girls who were now holding good jobs, from girls who were happily married. One came from a young woman who had become a school principal and who wrote: "Think, Sister, I'll be giving the address at commencement this year—the principal's address."

There were marriages at the convent, blessed by the Church, and several of their girls had been professed among the Magdalens with the Good Shepherd nuns.

When, in the spring of 1923, Mother Mary went to Trinidad, Archbishop Dowling asked if her community would take on the work of the government Industrial School for Girls. It had been in the charge of the French Dominicans sisters who already had an orphanage and leper colony in their charge and could no longer keep the work of the industrial school, since their members were needed for the increasing needs of their other tasks.

It was a fine place, with large buildings, cool and pleasant, a good garden and a productive farm. Mother Mary agreed to take it in charge and sent for some sisters to come immediately from England. She wanted them to come before the French sisters left so that they could learn methods from them. They were all greatly impressed by the charm of these French women, their dignity and beautiful manners, their kindly ways with the girls in their charge.

Over the years Mother Mary was to spend by far the greater share of her time in the United States although every year, or at least every other year, she managed to visit Trinidad or England or both.

She had announced her intention of applying for United States citizenship and so had to spend considerable time there. She had grown fond of the country. She liked the big heartedness of American people and the broad free spirit there. Then, too, it was beginning to be apparent that the location in England would have to be given up, because plans for the new Dominican church showed that the land on which Corpus Christi House stood would be needed. Citizenship in America seemed the natural thing for the increasing number of members who came to work in that country. In fact, for a time it was thought that America would provide a headquarters for the community.

Though the numbers of the community were still small in the United States, there was continuous demand for their services. They could not accept many of the offers. But they did accept, when in January of 1925, Bishop Francis Kelley of Oklahoma City asked them to take up visitation and census work in his see city. Four sisters covered this work, and it was no light task. It took three years to complete it. The sisters made over eighteen thousand visits, and incidentally gave instruction to thousands of children and adults. Lapsed Catholics were brought back to the Church; marriages were validated and many children were baptized. When the sisters had completed the census in Oklahoma City, they began a similar one in Tulsa.

Some of their friends feared that perhaps the sisters would not be received, to put it mildly, with politeness in some of the houses at whose doors they knocked. This proved a vain fear. Afterwards the sisters said they could remember at most ten houses where they had met with rudeness—"just enough to spur us on to fresh efforts and send us to ring the next door bell with renewed resolve."

Often the census taking had happy results. The sight of sisters at the door would stir memories of childhood and Sunday Mass, and sometimes very sad stories were poured out to the sympathetic sisters. There were several occasions when people who were not Catholic invited them in to talk. The census, which was supposedly purely for Catholics, resulted in several conversions.

In that same year Bishop Duffy of Grand Island, Nebraska, asked whether Mother Mary could send a few sisters to work on the Mexican mission at Scotts Bluff. In December on the great feast of the Indians, that of Our Lady of Guadeloupe, Sister Josephine and Sister Columba came to take charge. A little later Sister Mercedes came there as superior.

The sisters, who had read a good deal about the troubles of the Mexicans in their own land and the unhappy things the Church was enduring there, had been at first uneasy about this mission and the people. It did not take long for them to learn that their misgivings had been vain ones.

There was no doubt that the Mexicans they worked with were very poor. Their homes were often merely unplastered shacks, but the people who lived in them had always a certain dignity about them. The father was head of the house; the children very definitely honored their parents. They had to work when they were far too young, that was true; it was also true that these people were a happy and united group. They were people with a deep faith too. In almost every house was a little altar, even in the smallest and most crowded, and before it the families knelt to recite the rosary.

The children proved charming. It was especially delightful to watch the care the small boys took of their sisters, even when the latter were older and bigger. They were a people who loved their families. They were also a people who went to church, attending faithfully the tiny churches which dotted that area and which Bishop Duffy called his Little Prairie Cathedrals.

To some extent the Mexican population was a floating

one. When there was lack of employment in the beet fields they went back to Mexico. Mission work, too, had its definite dates. From early June to late autumn the whole family was in the fields, working from the time of planting to the harvesting of the beets. So the sisters' work began with early fall and ended in May with First Communions. It was a day greatly loved by the Mexicans, who flocked to watch the small communicants on this great day of their lives.

The sisters on the Mexican mission learned to love these people who placed so great a price on their faith. All along the sixty miles of the North Platte Valley which was their territory, they grew to know their gentleness and courtesy and devotion. They were well aware of the accusations against these people: that they loved the sacramentals more than the sacraments. The sisters felt this showed a great misunderstanding on the part of those who spoke thus.

It was very true that the Mexicans loved their rosaries and their statues, but one reason was that these were familiar things to them. Their difficulties with the matter of going to church and of making use of the sacraments often arose from their inability to understand the language spoken by those about them, and the absence of priests of their own nationality. Then, too, they were often too poor to be able to go to a church which was at a great walking distance.

In the whole valley there was no parochial school. The sisters who knew Spanish taught the little ones in that language and taught in English the older children who went to the public schools.

In some towns the sisters were obliged to teach the

Mexican and the American children in separate classes, but in others all the children came to the same classes and got along very well with each other. In some of the churches Mexicans were not made to feel very welcome; in others they furnished the music for the American choirs by playing their violins.

It hurt the sisters to see how pitifully little these gentle people from the South had. Once a doctor told a Mexican mother to put her sick boy out in the sun in his bed. She did. The bed was two boxes with a thin rug over them, another equally thin over him. It was little wonder the sisters wrote to their friends: "You can't send us anything which is not needed."

One day a priest came to Mother Mary with a story as sad as it was typical. He had just opened the door for Mass when a woman came up to him, looking very tired, and held out to him a tiny baby. She wanted it baptized, she made him understand; it was very ill. One look showed the priest that the child was close to death, and he was right. Hardly had he baptized the little mite when he saw it had died. He could not speak. He put the baby back in the mother's arms silently and saw that she too realized it was dead.

She said nothing. She walked to the altar and held the little body high as if she were offering it to God. Only later did the priest learn that the baby was just four days old and that the young mother had walked eight miles to have it baptized, knowing how sick it was.

"She was weeping when she told me the story," he said, "and I am very willing to tell you, Mother Mary, that when she was finished, I was weeping with her."

For a long time the greatest difficulty on the Mexican

mission had been the matter of transportation. There were always kindly people willing to take the sisters from one little town to another and from one cabin to another down the bumpy lanes, but they hated to ask it too often. Yet sometimes it was the only way they could carry out the work they had been sent to do.

Then one day a friend gave the sisters an old Dodge, which Sister Josephine promptly named Raimondo. This made things easier for them—that is, easier when the car could be persuaded to run. The roads were very rough often. In fact, sometimes they could not be called roads at all, for they were only remnants of old Indian trails and one had to be careful to watch its traces. Even if the houses to be visited were only eight miles apart, it took thirty miles of driving to get there sometimes, so twisted was the routes. It was on visits like these that they learned how hard life can be in a place where the only food available was what could be grown around the shacks, where there was no chance for medical help and often no spiritual help either.

Sister Josephine had grown as fond of her Mexicans as she had once been of her Trinidadians. And she had a special affection for the cantankerous old car, about which she talked as if the Dodge had been human. It was very obvious, she said, not long after Raimondo had become theirs, that he hated above all things catechism classes; he made that clear by the noises he emitted and the way he would often refuse to budge at all. Now and then he had to be urged into a garage before he stopped entirely and the garage man, who was used to him, would look him over with assumed surprise.

"Where you find Noah's Ark?" he would ask jestingly.

But Sister Josephine defended her Raimondo. "Just the thing to carry a quiver full of Mexican children or old clothes or potatoes to distribute," she would reply tartly to criticism.

With whacks and thumps Raimondo could usually be persuaded to get going again, at least to the next town. And it was very true that he never failed to get them to classes and home to the convent, but the trips never lost the excitement of suspense.

It was well that the sisters had a good sense of humor. It was often needed, for the work they were doing was very difficult; it was, in fact, pioneer work. In one area the priest told them, "They are scattered all around here. Whatever you do will be all right with me," and so left them to their own devices.

In some little settlements a single shack might yield five or six children, ragged and untaught. If a sister asked them to make the sign of the cross, a child was likely to stare without understanding. Once a mother made frantic signals behind Sister's back to show them. "Of a stupidity they are," she said in Spanish and was surprised to find Sister Josephine answering her in that language.

Reluctantly the reason came out. Her husband did not want the children instructed. He didn't like the American padres.

In the end few parents refused the sisters. After weeks of preparation the priest came for the first confessions in one of the little shacks, and then came the ceremony of First Communion in the nearest little church. Fathers and mothers often came too, some only to watch their offspring, but others to make a long deferred duty—"and in a sensible language" said one to Sister Josephine. For the priests who came on such occasions could nearly always speak Spanish.

On First Communion days the tiny church was a busy spot. Babies lay asleep on the benches. Three and four year olds ran up and down the aisle. To the altar rail came children from five years old, wide-eyed and sober as the old pastor bent over each in turn and spoke the words which are the same for king and slave, for the child of wealth and the Mexican child of the northern beet fields.

It was with a fine sense of accomplishment that after such an event the sisters turned homeward. They used to feel that one reason they succeeded in their efforts—and sometimes against great odds—was that they had used during all their hours of instruction the advice of Father Vaughan to the motor mission workers in England: "Make the little children's religion not a formal business but a love affair between themselves and Jesus."

The Mexican mission had produced a fine example of the deep courtesy which the children showed to the sisters who taught them. Sister Josephine had by that time learned to speak their language quite well, having learned it chiefly by the unusual method of procuring a Spanish Bible and teaching herself by comparing it with the English version. The mission was also on occasion apt to produce an ignorance as deep as the courtesy.

"How many Gods are there?" asked Sister Josephine of one class.

"There is one God," came back the assured answer.

"How many persons are there in God?" she asked, and there was a dead silence. Finally one small boy spoke up. "How many would the Madre prefer?" he asked politely.

Since the Madre evidently wanted them to give the answer themselves, a small girl spoke up. "Would two be enough?"

Sister said she really preferred three and held up three fingers to show how many she meant. Then in Spanish she gave their names—El Padre, El Hijo, El Spirito Santo.

"But that is four, Madre," objected one boy, and Sister explained patiently that the last Person had a double name. This explanation brought a chorus of voices, "Poor Padre, poor Hijo, they have only one name!"

After this wave of sympathy for the Deity, Sister Josephine explained that God is a spirit and cannot be seen even though he is ever present. Inside each child was a spirit called his soul.

Small Pedro, who rarely spoke, was moved to rise and, his hand on his chest, he said gravely, "You are right, Madre. Many times I have felt Him here."

# NINE

In 1924 MOTHER MARY HAD MADE A VISITATION OF THE house at Trinidad and among the plans she carried out while she was there was the establishing of a new group of tertiaries. Among the colored girls with whom the sisters had worked were some who felt they had a vocation to the religious life. At the request of the Archbishop, it was now planned to train a group of them at the Trinidad house. If all went well, they would renew their profession each year but would make no final vows. Their dress was to be a white tunic and veil and a black cape.

When Mother Mary came again in 1926, it was to preside at the first of these entrants, Sister Mary of the Sacred Heart, who had come from an island near Grenada. She was professed as an oblate. The two years had shown that the plan was working well, even though at first some of the islanders had discouraged the congregation about them, saying these girls would not prove stable members. It was true that there had been some failures at first, since there was no tradition of religious life among them. On this account the training period had been lengthened.

The recruits who remained were adapting themselves well, and it was evident that they would prove fine missionaries for their own people. This was in line with the mind of the Church and with the expressed hope of more than one of the popes. Native vocations were to be encouraged, and Mother Mary, when she left Trinidad, was happy to know that a group of colored girls were almost ready to make their first vows.

She went next to England, to their house in Leicester, where, as in many other parts of the country, the war had caused a great shortage of housing. Young workers who came to the city often found it impossible to get decent lodgings. A part of Corpus Christi House had been opened to them. Some came to stay for only a few nights, some for months, until they found a permanent home.

They were of every profession—doctors, clerks, nurses, teachers. Occasionally a girl came for convalescent care after leaving the hospital. Some came for week ends so that they might go to Mass since they lived far from a church. There were unemployed there too for whom the sisters were able to find work. They even had a runaway whom they persuaded to go back home. Some who came were not Catholic and were ignorant of all things about the Church. One guest was overheard to say to a newcomer, when a bell rang, "That's to call the saints together in the chapel."

There were several permanent guests at Corpus Christi, one of them Miss Annie Fitzwilliams, eighty-two years old, a tiny lady, cheerful and pleasant in manner, very dignified, though she was so bent that she had to look up sideways when she spoke to anyone. Her many years had not dimmed her faculties in the least; she was so bright and chipper that the sisters thought she looked exactly like a robin redbreast. Her brief stay with the sisters was one of devoted communion with her Lord, both at the altar and in her heart. She never missed Mass though it grew increasingly difficult for her to come downstairs.

When Mother Mary came that year to the English house it was to learn that Miss Fitzwilliams had only recently died. She had had a stroke which paralyzed her but left her able to speak. She asked that word of her condition be sent to her only surviving relative, a religious. And now the sisters learned why they had always had the feeling that their guest was a religious.

When she was a young girl, so her sister said, she had wanted to be a Carmelite and was ready to enter when her mother died and left her a baby sister to care for. She put aside her own hopes, brought up the child left in her charge, educated her and saw her enter the religious life. By that time she was too old to enter herself, and so she lived the rest of her long life as a "nun" in the world.

They had dressed her, the sisters told Mother Mary, in the white dress she had kept carefully put away for her burial; its yellowed lace showed how long she had treasured it. The sisters said the Office of the Dead around her as if she had been a religious. For none of their other guests had it occurred to the sisters to do this. For her it seemed right. They showed Mother Mary the one memento of her left: her ivory crucifix, worn but very lovely.

Mother Mary told the English sisters about another old lady, this one in the States, with whom she had from time to time been corresponding. This had its beginning in Mother Mary's idea of forming a group of Adorers to pray for the Corpus Christi community, and who would form a sort of auxiliary. She wrote to several retired school teachers, among them a Miss Eliza Murphy of Boston. Pleasant letters were exchanged and finally a rather startling one arrived. After saying that Mother Mary's letters had meant a great deal to her, for she was a lonely old lady, she felt she ought to tell her that for many years she had not been a practicing Catholic—"and doubtless you will not want to write again to such a person."

Mother Mary wrote immediately and said she was sending her a little friend to represent her since she could not come herself; it was the story of the recently canonized Thérèse of Lisieux. Some weeks later a letter came from Miss Murphy: she was trying hard to get back into the Church, but she had been so long away. She had forgotten so much, she said. She was so old she could not go the long distance to the nearest church. For the time being she was making no further attempts, but she loved the book and was beginning to read it for the second time.

Mother Mary begged her sisters to pray hard for the return of the wanderer, and said she would write Miss Murphy that the whole community was praying for her homecoming.

During her stay in England, Mother Mary received a letter from Canon Taylor, who was the English translator of the life of Thérèse of Lisieux. He invited Mother Mary to visit the Shrine of the Two Queens at the little town of Carfin near Glasgow in Scotland, where he was pastor. She accepted and he wrote again: he had another gift for her which he would give her when she came.

From Glasgow the train took her the few miles to the town of Motherwell, and there people sent by Canon Taylor drove her the few miles to Carfin. "You will find Carfin an unusual place in that every person is a Catholic," the driver told her.

It was a plain little town. The single street was lined with miners' cottages and at the end of the street was the rectory and Canon Taylor waiting at the door to welcome her.

He took her to the Shrine, telling her its history as they walked along. The miners of Carfin had built it themselves in honor of Our Lady after some of them had gone on the Scottish National Pilgrimage to Lourdes in 1920. On their return they announced they wanted to build a grotto like the one they had seen. The work was placed under the auspices and protection of Thérèse of Lisieux.

Mother Mary reached the grotto in time for the afternoon devotions. She was amazed to see how many people were there. It was a very simple service. Canon Taylor gave out the general intentions of the parish, of the pilgrims to the grotto and of the Corpus Christi visitor. Then followed a decade of the rosary, the litany of Our Lady, and a remembrance of the dead.

Late in the afternoon, at a new and not yet completed shrine of Saint Thérèse, the novena prayers were recited and then Canon Taylor said to the people, "Gather up your intentions and lay them at the feet of the Little Flower to offer to the great Queen."

In the evening another meeting was held, and this was so hugely attended that the crowd flowed into the street. What amazed Mother Mary was to see so many men, and young men at that. Benediction in the church followed; the steady stream of people who poured across the square, so many that a considerable number could not get inside, but loud speakers allowed them to hear the ceremony and Father Taylor's words. He said that all who wished might venerate the relics of Saint Thérèse; they were to come to the altar rail, especially the sick. A thousand and more people streamed to the rail, and the sick, she noticed, pointed to eyes or chest or heart before they knelt to kiss the relic.

Everything at the Carfin shrine, Mother Mary was told, was built by the voluntary work of the Carfin miners. Much was still incomplete. There was a strike going on at the time and the men were out of work, but they were not loafing; they were putting their time in to the completing of the grotto and the shrine.

When Mother Mary was leaving the next day, Canon Taylor produced the second gift he had promised her. He gave her a check. "This is to take you to Lisieux," he told her. "She is sending you there herself for this is her own money," and he pointed out that the check was drawn to the "Little Flower Account." The money doubtless came from the sale of the book which he had translated, for it was well known that he had spent no penny of it on himself.

So Mother Mary Ellerker was at last to see the actual

place where had lived and prayed and died the saint to whom she had given her devotion long before her canonization. The fact that her own sister Ethel had been for a brief time a member of the company of Carmel no doubt drew her; but it was also true that even in the early days at Leicester, and earlier, it was Thérèse Martin about whom she had told the children in her classes.

She reached Lisieux late in the morning and went to a Mass said by a priest pilgrim. Later, visiting the shops she was overwhelmed by the hundreds of objects for sale —"anything which can bear a figure or a picture of the Little Flower," she wrote home.

There was no hostel for religious, she learned, but a girl in one of the shops took her to a private house close to the Carmel; there Madame Maria had a spotlessly clean room to let. When Mother Mary leaned from her window, she found she could see into the open door of the Carmel chapel and saw near the altar rail a statue of Saint Thérèse. It was as if she was welcoming her in her gracious way, and Mother Mary hoped she would find great graces there.

In the afternoon she went to the Saint's childhood home and saw the garden she had loved. She had the feeling that she had seen it all before, so familiar was it to her from reading her own book. She came back to the Carmel in time for vespers. The sisters beyond the grille were saying the Divine Office, and very beautifully, every voice giving its best to God. Mother Mary thanked Him as she knelt close to the altar, because they of Corpus Christi were able, too, to offer that sacrifice of praise.

In the afternoon she went to see the relics, and then to talk with one of the religious in the parlor. Mother Mary told her that she was bringing many intentions to Lisieux, but especially one intention of her own, and the religious promised to tell Thérèse's sister Mére Agnes, about it, and then the whole community would pray that God would give her the light to know His will in regard to her intention.

Mother Mary loved everything at Lisieux and this love extended to the people she met there. They were so different in rank and condition, so united in love for the young saint. Once, while she was kneeling in prayer in the chapel, she heard outside the sounds of laughter. The laughter ceased suddenly and three young French officers came in, walked to the shrine, gave a military salute to the statue, stood there rigidly for a few moments, saluted again and walked out.

Thousands of ex-votos lined the chapel walls and the two high pillars were covered with them from floor to ceiling, many of them military decorations placed there in thanksgiving for Saint Thérèse's protection during the great war.

After a peaceful night in the little room, Mass at six next morning and Benediction, she had to leave. She found it hard to go away, but she comforted herself by remembering that Corpus Christi houses, in the Old World and the New, were, she felt sure, under the little Saint's protection. She would take care of them because they were small and poor and unimportant. That was why they had in a very special way a claim on the love and patronage of the saint of little things. And they were rich in one thing, as she had been, love for the Blessed Sacrament and for the old and the sick whom God loved.

The intention which Mother Mary had left with Saint

Thérèse was a very important one. It might greatly affect the whole future of the community which she had founded and which she loved.

For twenty years they had been working in the vineyard. Chiefly it had been under Dominicans that they had worked. Father McNabb, their friend and advisor and teacher, had trained them well in religion. They had worked under Dominican bishops in Trinidad, and their great friend in the New World, who had, in fact, asked them to come there, was another Dominican, Bishop McNicholas.

It was also true that during all those years they had been in an anomalous position. They had followed the tertiary rule of Saint Dominic as best they could. They were, however, under no special obedience to anyone save in ordinaries of the dioceses in which they worked, and they had no status as religious. They had been founded under the Bishop of Nottingham in 1908, when he expressly asked them to come to work for him. Most fortunate of all their Dominican connections had been the fact that, during their first years in religion, Father McNabb had been close to them. And it had been chiefly due to Father Wilberforce in London and Father McNabb in Leicester that they had become Dominican tertiaries in the first place.

There was little doubt that during those years the Dominicans had stood by them and still did. Several times Father Cormier, then prior general, had sent them encouraging letters. In 1924 the New York provincial, Father Meagher, wrote to her, addressing her as Mother Mary Ellerker, O.S.D. He spoke of the fact that he knew she was then petitioning for an approval from the Holy

See as a lay institute, and he spoke highly of the excellent work of her sisters in Duluth and Trinidad.

From London Father Bede Jarrett had added his approval to the step. He had long watched their work, he wrote—"active, eager, alert, and thorough." Then, too, he and his associates had always felt a certain security about the future of the Corpus Christi group because they had continued to say the Divine Office: "It is so easy to become absorbed in the social energies of Catholic good works as to lose the deeper essence which alone can make these good works endure." He added a sentence which Mother Mary was often to repeat to her sisters in the future: "The more active and missionary the Order, the greater is its need for the Divine Office, not the less need."

From the provincial of the Irish Province, Father Finbar Ryan, came a letter, also supporting the petition they were offering to the Holy See for canonical approval. Like Father Jarrett, he spoke of his delight in knowing that the Divine Office was part of their daily prayer, for he felt the recital of this was the best way to prepare for the external work which they carried on. To these letters Archbishop Keating of Liverpool added his word of commendation for the Corpus Christi sisters.

They were specifically asking Rome if they might become a pontifical lay institute. They sent with this request all the Dominican letters they had received as references —all from men well known in the Church. In their favor was the fact that they had houses in more than one diocese, that they had been founded by the Bishop of Nottingham, that as early as 1911 the General of the Dominican Order had sent them a letter praising their work, that in 1912 Pius X had sent them his blessing and encouraged them to persevere, writing to them as a "society of women whose members imitate the manner of life of religious living in community under the government of superiors according to approved constitutions but without the usual three vows of religion." And in 1914 they had received formal affiliation with the Dominican Order as tertiaries living in community.

Despite all the letters, written by men of high responsibility, despite all the detail of their work and the fact that they were continuously growing, the hoped-for recognition as a lay institute did not come from Rome. It was thought that the group was too small and too young. It was felt that with an increasing number of members and houses they would acquire a greater stability and be in a position to take vows. Then their request would be again considered.

Their friends were almost as disappointed as were the sisters. Father Finbar Ryan wrote what all of them said in varying ways: "I am very disappointed about the refusal. In a way, it may be fortunate since you will work all the harder to set your foundations deep and wide." He added that he was happy to know they maintained adoration of the Blessed Sacrament: "It will be always for you a source of great sanctity."

From the time of that refusal in 1924, Mother Mary and her associates had spoken more than once of taking the three vows of religion and becoming a regular group of religious rather than mere tertiaries. More and more, too, the thought of Carmel had been in Mother Mary's thoughts. The sisters had for some time been using the

Carmelite Manual for novices and had been reading the life of Thérèse Martin, so recently canonized.

Now, after her visit to Lisieux, Mother Mary began to realize how much they had been living the spirit of Carmel; how for some years their lives had been tending in the direction of that Order. As several priors had pointed out in letters, the community had always made an effort to keep in view the need for contemplation, for solitude, and for the liturgy, even though their work was in the world. More and more Mother Mary was realizing that the motto of Carmel was the basis of their apostolic life.

There were smaller things which had pointed in the direction of Carmel. The day on which Bishop Brindle had asked her to open the school and the social work had been the feast of Our Lady of Mount Carmel. Even before that, she had read and been deeply impressed by the life of Thérèse Martin and had long cherished her words. To some extent she had used the *Story of a Soul* even in the novitiate. Then too their community devotions were those of Carmel—devotion to the Child Jesus, to solitude and their own cells, to making the Divine Office their first and chief prayer.

Mother Mary began to feel a quiet conviction growing in her that, as she wrote to one of the sisters, "We shall find we have been living the spirit of Carmel all along. I do not mean in its perfection, but that our life has been along that line, and always with an effort to keep in view the need for contemplation, for solitude, for the liturgy and for this to express itself in the apostolic life as our realization of the motto of Carmel."

She came back to the United States, after a brief stay in England, and spoke of these ideas to her sisters there, as she had spoken to the sisters in other houses. Still uncertain what to do, for they had no money or powerful friends, they decided to appeal to Saint Thérèse herself. They wrote a letter and placed it under her statue: would she take up the matter, see to things in Rome and, if it was the will of God, help to bring about the fruition of their hope—to be a true recognized congregation within the Church.

A trip to Chicago took Mother Mary to the famous shrine of the Little Flower there, and she saw almost as many of Saint Thérèse's personal belongings there as there were at Lisieux. Later she met Father Diether, Carmelite provincial of Chicago, and, when she talked with him of this half-formed intention of her community, he offered to help. He said that his order had been anxious to see active branches of the Carmelites established in the United States. He would take up the matter for them in Rome. A few weeks later he wrote her that Father Magennis, Prior General of his Order, had received their petition in a fatherly way and promised to expedite their cause.

Among some of the Dominicans with whom they had been so long associated, there was surprise when this move became known, but others felt it was a reasonable move. The Archbishop of Trinidad, a Dominican, and their oldest and best friend among the Dominicans did not feel sorrow at the news. From across the seas, Father Vincent McNabb sent his message: "May Our Lady of Mount Carmel make you at home in her Order."

On February 7, 1927, a decree of the Roman curia joined to the Third Order of Carmelites the group which had been known as the Dominican Tertiaries of Corpus Christi, and who would now be known as Corpus Christi Carmelites. Rome had designated Port of Spain as the head house; it was the only one of their houses which had been canonically erected. There were thirty-one sisters in the congregation at the time.

The letter from the Prior General which announced this ended with a prayer that the Father of all mercies might consecrate this aggregation and that Our Lady of Mount Carmel would prosper it.

Word of the granting of the decree reached the sisters on a feast very important to Carmelites, that of Saint Elijah, or, in the more often used Latin, Saint Elias, who had long been regarded by many as the founder of the Order. The letter bearing the document reached the sisters on the feast of Saint Dominic, and this made them feel that he was still with them.

The rescript of canonical erection was published by the Archbishop of Port of Spain, in November of 1928. At the same time the constitutions were being drawn up in Rome especially for the Corpus Christi Carmelites.

The order with which the sisters were now affiliated considered as its founder the prophet Elias, and this ancient and cherished tradition was fully sanctioned by the Church. In the Vatican, among the statues of founders of religious orders that of Elias bears the inscription: "The Order of Carmel has erected this to the holy prophet, Elias, its founder."

The early fathers of the Church honored him. Saint Jerome said that, if the sources of monastic life were to be sought in Scripture, then Elias, who lived nine hundred years before Christ was born, could be considered the chief source. Saint Augustine, Saint John Chrysostom and Saint Gregory all hailed him. Pope Clement VIII in 1604 wrote to the Carmelites: "Distinguished as you are by humility, poverty, abnegation, you show you are disciples of your father Saint Elias, founder of your institute."

In the Bible Elias appeared first when he accused the wicked king Achab, and told of a famine to come. "As the Lord liveth, the God of Israel in whose sight I stand," was his dramatic opening. The king became angry and would no doubt have killed him but God told Elias to "hide by the torrent of Carith" and "to drink of its waters"; He would send ravens to feed him. When the drouth which Elias had predicted came to pass, he was told to leave and go to Sarephtha where a widow would take care of him. The widow to whom he came was as poor as he; she had a bit of flour and a little oil and it would be the last food she had for herself and her little son. But she offered him a share of this and he accepted. From that meal there was no lack of oil and meal for them all, then and in the days to come. And, when the widow's little son died, Elias prayed to God to restore the child to life and He did.

The famine was still raging and Achab appealed to Elias, who told him to gather the people on Mount Carmel. He would himself speak to them and also to the false prophets among them. After his talk the rain came and the people rejoiced. The famine was over.

Elias meantime had remained on Mount Carmel to pray after the crowd had gone away. While he was there he noticed a little cloud rising from the sea and knew it was a holy sign. Long afterwards the Fathers of the

Church were to say it had been the figure of Our Lady.

At all events, Carmel had from antiquity been considered a holy mountain. It was one of a chain in northern Palestine. There Elias continued to live, at first alone, and later with the disciples who came to him. The mountain had great natural beauty. Along its sides were groves of all kinds, as well as orange and olive trees. No doubt from this vista of trees and flowers had come its name, for in Hebrew Carmel means a garden, a lovely slope. In the Scriptures the bride is likened to it because she is lovely as Carmel is lovely.

It is still a beautiful place. The English poet Pope wrote of it, "Carmel, thy flowery top perfumes the skies."

After the beginning of the Christian era the apostles came to talk with the disciples of Elias, for his sons had continued to live there after he left them for Heaven. When these "sons of the Prophet" heard the preaching of the new revelation, they became Christians too. On the spot where Elias a thousand years before had seen a little cloud rise from the sea, they built the first little chapel and dedicated it to the Virgin. From that time they were called the Brethren of Blessed Mary of Mount Carmel.

It was Elias who had spoken the words which form even today the motto of the Carmelite Order: "With zeal I have been zealous for the Lord God of hosts."

When he left them, Eliseus, his spiritual son, carried on his work. The number of the hermits increased and they began to spread to other areas and build new hermitages, not only through Palestine but in far countries. Always they lived the way of life which had begun at

Mount Carmel. In the twelfth century they decided it would be better to have one superior whom all would obey and they chose Berthold de Malifay, who had gone to Palestine with the French crusaders and there decided to enter the religious life. A century later Saint Albert Patriarch of Jerusalem, wrote a rule for the community.

By that time the Holy Land was in dire straits, for the Saracens had defeated the Christians. When the warriors returned home, the knights invited some of the monks to come with them to their own countries. One of these lands was England, where they soon spread and flourished.

In the thirteenth century Corpus Christi College was founded by them at Cambridge. To a monastery in Aylesford in Kent, Simon Stock came as a member of the Order. He had studied at Oxford and then had gone to Mount Carmel for some years. Like Elias, it was to Our Lady that he gave his special devotion. It was to him that she appeared with the scapular which the centuries have made famous.

# *TEN*

THE SAME YEAR WHICH SAW THE AFFILIATION OF THE Corpus Christi Sisters with Carmel saw the end of the house at Leicester. The priory, which owned the land and the house, needed space for its new church and the house had to be torn down.

There were no suitable places available at the time; the housing shortage was still acute. All the houses which were offered to the sisters were far beyond their means. With great reluctance the continuance of a house in England was, at least for the time being, given up. By March of the following year it was decided that the house which had been the second founded—the house in Trinidad—would be the one in which the ceremonies of affiliation were carried out.

On November 11, 1928, Archbishop Dowling had signed the decree of canonical erection which gave the group a religious status. Belmont Carmel became the first novitiate of the new group within the Carmelite Order and the site of the motherhouse.

On January 21, 1929, in Corpus Christi chapel, bright with lights and glowing with flowers, voices sang a welcome to the Archbishop as he and his attendants entered. It was a day which had long been awaited by the sisters, the day when, after twenty years, the Church publicly accepted their vows and placed them among her consecrated daughters.

The Archbishop asked the preparatory questions and then made a short address. He knew these religious well; he knew of their trials and their disappointments. He knew too what good work they had done for his people. He spoke to them of love, especially of the love of God.

The sermon over, Mother Mary went up to the sanctuary alone and, kneeling before him, pronounced her vows. Then she returned to her stall and one by one the sisters went to her and with their hands held in hers, vowed poverty, chastity and obedience. Then came the blessing of the scapular, the veil, the white mantle, the ring, the breviary. The sisters were to continue to wear the medal which they had worn from the beginning of their work. Then each knelt in turn before the Archbishop and received her habit.

The ceremonies ended with a Te Deum, which all sang, and Benediction of the Blessed Sacrament.

That evening the sisters studied very carefully the drawing of the Carmelite arms which had been given to them.

The motto recorded there was the one taken from the Book of Kings: "With zeal have I been zealous for the Lord God of hosts." Under the escutcheon was a mountain in brown and three gold crowns in a field of white. Over that a fiery sword over a crown.

The motto represented Mount Carmel, where the order was born and where it lived for centuries. The sword of Elias was poised over Mary's crown, showing loyalty for God and Our Lady. The three stars stood for the three eras in the Order's history. The brown and white reminded the members of the Order that it was Mary who gave them the brown habit.

From Trinidad Mother Mary went to her houses in America, and there the same ceremony was enacted. When she reached there she found another project on the way, one which in the future was to become the Francis Keens Home for the Aged.

At Kearney, Nebraska, there had been erected many years before, a group of flats, eight in number, which for a considerable time were considered excellent places in which to live. Close to them was a frame house where Mr. Keens, the owner, and his wife made their home. Now they had gone to live elsewhere. The flats were almost empty. Not only were they out of fashion but the neighborhood had changed.

When Mr. Keens came there one day to consider what to do with his property, the thought came to him that it was a pity these fine brick buildings should not be put to some use. Not long before he had passed a hospital which Franciscan sisters had in charge and he remembered that originally it had been an unused building. Why, he wondered, could not his flats be put to some use instead of being torn down, as he had planned doing.

He was a Protestant but it was to the parish priest that he went to discuss this idea, and from their conversation came the plan for the Keens Home. Since the Corpus Christi Sisters were already engaged in work in that state, they were asked to take the Home over if they possibly could. When Mother Mary was informed of this, she suggested that several of the sisters go to look it over and tell her what they thought of the proposition.

They found four sets of flats, each a separate unit but attached to each other. They saw that the smaller house would do for a convent and the others could be remodelled into one large unit; but where would one find the money for converting the flats, putting in a furnace, and furnishing it? One of the rules of the congregation was that of poverty, and the sisters had kept it well.

However, the report was sent to Mother Mary. In the end, after some hesitation, it was decided to accept. In the spring of 1929 three sisters would go there, live in the frame house and see what could be done about going further with plans for a home for the aged.

Sister Teresa, Sister Dolores and Sister Francis Paul were the pioneers. When they reached Kearney on March 6, they found to their delighted surprise that the Altar Society of the parish church had a fine lunch and hot coffee waiting for them. Linen and furniture, too, had been supplied and the sisters found that they would be very comfortable in their new home. They immediately began what they called "interior decorating," mostly painting and varnishing and paper hanging. Several weeks later they planted a garden. One afternoon when they were very busy putting in onion sets, they heard a taxi drive up and saw it deposit an elderly woman and then depart.

Sister Teresa shook the earth from her hands and went to greet the newcomer. It took only a few words to make it clear that she thought the new home was already taking guests and she had come to stay. She was so old and so tired that no one had the heart to tell her the truth: that nothing was ready to receive old people, not even the house they were some day to live in. They took furniture from their own rooms, fixed one for her, and the old lady retired happily, unaware that she was sleeping in the bed of one of the sisters.

One small room in the house had been set aside as a chapel. There in April Father Munstermann said the first Mass. To the sisters' joy he said he would leave there the Blessed Sacrament.

The remodeling of the flats began. They were to be connected into one large building. An oil furnace was ordered. Mr. Keens came often to see how things were progressing and always with gifts, or the promise of gifts —a gas stove, a water heater and tank; and he had the grounds landscaped. Before long the sisters would be able to add more old people to the one who had come so unexpectedly and who had been with them ever since.

Meantime another work had been undertaken in the autumn of 1929. It was in the east, and a very different one from those which had previously engaged the attention of the sisters.

The Carmelite Fathers in Middletown, New York, asked if several of the Corpus Christi Carmelites could come to do the catering and cooking for the junior seminary there, and also do catechetical work and parish visiting. Mother Mary accepted and with two sisters came to set up the work.

The Fathers met them and brought them in their own car to the house which was to be their Carmel. It was an excellent house. They walked into a spacious hall. On the left was the room which was the chapel and which they entered in their white cloaks singing the Magnificat. They noted the fine floors, the paneled wall, the oak rafters in the rooms downstairs. Upstairs were good bedrooms.

When they were getting ready to retire, however, they found something lacking. There was no bedding. The trunks with this had not yet arrived. They were resigned to sleeping in bathrobes, but Mother Mary suddenly remembered one trunk of oddments which she had had sent on from Trinidad and which might have what they needed.

When they opened it they found it held some bedclothes. Everything had been packed away for a long time and was redolent of the sweet grass in which it had been packed. They looked in surprise at what they had found—the bedclothes of Sister Mary Magdalene and Sister Teresa Vincent from the old Leicester days.

Mother Mary looked at them lovingly. "Isn't it just like those two to have come with us on a new foundation and then have taken care to give us what we needed," she said.

In the morning they prepared the chapel for their first Mass and then worked hard, cleaning and unpacking. In the afternoon came a wire. It was from Miss Murphy in Boston who was sending them some of her own furniture, including a piano.

She and Mother Mary had never lost sight of each other. She was still trying to find her way back into the Church. She was much nearer now and, since they had a house close by where she could stay if she wished, Mother Mary decided to ask her to come to stay with them. In answer she had written thanking her; she was now winding up her business affairs, packing up everything at her home of years, all a difficult job for a woman over seventy.

The sisters had written offering to take some of her furniture and this, she wrote, was even now on the way. It was more than possible that she would soon come too.

The next letter was full of hesitation. Evidently she was finding it hard to make up her mind to come to a convent. She said she doubted if she would ever get to Corpus Christi.

She did come, but not until several more years had gone by.

On their second day in Middletown several of the sisters who had gone out for supplies, reported that the town had narrow winding streets and looked very much like an English town. That afternoon Ursuline sisters came to call. They had an academy and a parochial school in the city and they told the newcomers about their work and invited them to Sunday dinner. In the evening the Prior of the Carmelite community came to take the sisters to Benediction in the college chapel. It was a lovely ceremony, the men's voices singing the well-known words in Latin cadences.

Next day a letter came from Miss Murphy: the vans would no doubt reach Middletown as soon as the letter did. She had also sent a box of apples and hoped, she added darkly, they would reach Middletown uneaten.

On Sunday morning they walked home from Mass, wondering why Miss Murphy's vans had not arrived the day before. Sister Teresa, remembering Miss Murphy's suspicions, had unhappy visions of the driver and his assistant sitting somewhere along the road, playing the piano and eating the apples.

When the sisters neared their home they saw something standing in front of it—the missing van. They looked at it with mixed emotions, for they had hoped to do no hard work on that day. But they hurried into the house to put down old pieces of carpet to save their fine oak floors. They waited for the men to bring in what the van contained. They were not, however, ready for the amount which it disgorged—chairs, tables, bedsteads, wardrobes, and also the box of apples. Last of all came the piano, a good one they noted, a Kohler and Campbell. Miss Murphy had indeed been generous.

In June of 1931 the first General Chapter of the congregation was held in Middletown. It was a very happy occasion, for some of the members who came as delegates had not seen each other for years. It was a wonderful reunion. Sister Gertrude and Sister St. John landed in New York from Trinidad on June first and reached Middletown in time for the feast of Corpus Christi. Others of the old hands followed soon—Sister Teresa and Sister Francis Paul from Kearney, Sister Mary Augustine and Sister Patricia from Duluth, Sister Mercedes from Scottsbluff. The house overflowed. In fact, the Middletown sisters turned over their convent to the delegates and moved to a cottage which the Carmelite Fathers put at their disposal. They also loaned them an organ for the chapel. It was a considerable community which sang the joyous "Lauda Sion" at High Mass on the feast of Corpus Christi.

Bishop Dunn of the New York archdiocese presided over the chapter. The Carmelite provincial, Father D. L. Flanagan, came with him from New York. At the election Mother Mary was re-elected as Mother General. Councillors and other officers were elected. A Te Deum of thanksgiving was sung before the Blessed Sacrament exposed on the little altar.

This day the Corpus Christi Sisters ranked with their great days of the past years—the day the rescript of their affiliation came from Rome, the day of canonical erection, the day of their first vows.

In the circular which Mother Mary sent to all the houses she spoke of the fact that though, in the spirit of Carmel, the congregation must follow more and more closely the Little Way of Saint Thérèse, they must remember that this would not in any way bring about a break in the continuity of their love and devotion to the Blessed Sacrament, which had been the chief reason they had come together at Leicester in the beginning.

She wrote also that the Carmel at Kearney had just been honored with a visit from the Apostolic Delegate, Archbishop Fumasoni-Biondi who, speaking of their new affiliation, said he felt it had been for the good of the congregation and that it had been the will of God. A letter had come from Father Hilary Doswald, assistant to the Carmelite General, praising their work. And from Lisieux had come a letter from Saint Thérèse's sister,

Mère Agnès, asking the new congregation to follow closely in their saint's little way.

One sadness marred the happy occasion, a totally unexpected death. During the years since Mother Mary's own mother and sister had died, there had been no death in the community. That summer another was added to their members in Heaven.

The Chapter had closed and the sisters were preparing to leave for their houses, among them Sister Francis Paul, who was all packed up to go back to Kearney, happy because she was taking back with her all manner of small gifts. She had just been elected Fourth Councillor at the Chapter. She was with the rest at Mass and then she went to her room. When Mother Mary went there to ask her something she found her lying in her bed and was shocked to find her dead.

Everything in the room was in perfect order, her white mantle which she had worn at chapel hanging on its hook, her scapular and veil carefully arranged. Her eyes were closed and she lay as if asleep. The doctor said she must have had a heart attack and died almost instantly. It was Sunday and word of the death came to the Carmelite Fathers as they were ready to set out for the small missions they served on that day.

All said their Masses for Sister Francis Paul's soul. It was the first time the Corpus Christi Sisters realized fully what it meant to be an actual part of an Order. All day fathers and brothers passed in and out of the little chapel praying. On Monday they said the Office of the Dead about her coffin. On Tuesday the Provincial came from New York and said Mass in the chapel. Then Sister Francis Paul's body was taken to St. Albert's College and in their chapel the Carmelite Fathers and Brothers sang the Requiem Mass.

In January of 1932 the Corpus Christi Carmelites prepared to make their first perpetual vows. Though it was true that there were as yet not fifty members in the congregation, they already formed a very cosmopolitan group. There were representatives of Europe, America, Asia and Africa among them. Especially with the expressed hope of more than one of the popes, colored vocations were encouraged among them. As yet their group was not an actual part of the community, but the time was drawing near when they would be ready to be accepted as regular members. There had been failures in the group, but successes too. Several years before, five oblates had made their first vows and others would soon do so. In general their life followed that of the sisters who made perpetual vows. Each day in choir they recited the Office of the Dead, as their special contribution to aid for the holy souls. They were being especially trained to do catechetical work and visit the poor on the island. After a few years it was planned to draft them gradually into the Corpus Christi congregation, and they would then make their vows after the usual time in the novitiate. The Carmel at Lisieux was very interested in the colored oblates and promised to pray for them all.

The ceremony in 1932 marked the end of a long search and a final attainment. The evening before it took place in Trinidad, where Mother Mary had come a few days before, she was telling the community at recreation a story which this day had brought to her mind, something which happened long ago in England.

She was talking with a Carmelite religious and the voice behind the grille told her that she was a convert, too, and that her conversion had come about in an odd way. She was going through Westminster Cathedral in London, merely as a sightseer, and she came at the beginning of the service of Benediction. In those few moments the Faith had come to her, she said, and that was all that was granted her—that flash of faith. From then on she had to find her way into the Church by herself and by the ordinary means. There had been that one illumination for the spirit, that one light for the way. From there she had found her way step by step, but only because she had walked where the one gleam of light had showed her how to go. "And that is the Carmelite way," she had said to Clara Ellerker.

The Dominican Archbishop Dowling again presided at this ceremony as he had at earlier ones. The community felt a deep affection for this prelate and an equally deep thankfulness for the way he had guided them through the years. In fact, it was to him that Mother Mary had gone before she made her final decision and it was he who said to her, "I think, Mother, that Our Lady is calling you to her."

Others were there on that day—their chaplain, Dr. Meenan, Father O'Neill, the Dominican vicar provincial, and Father Sebastian Weber, the Benedictine who had given their retreat of preparation for this event. Around Mother General were some of the first members of the Corpus Christi group, among them Sister Gertrude from the Leicester group.

Mother Mary knelt before the Archbishop as she had knelt there three years before. But this time the vow was stronger; this time it was "unto death." Back in her stall, she waited while the others came to her and made into her hands the promise which made them Carmelites for life. Then they were vested in the long black veil of Carmel. The Te Deum with which the ceremony ended was soon over but in their hearts the lovely words still rang: "We praise Thee, O God."

A few days later Mother Mary left Trinidad for Nebraska where another old friend presided at the same ceremony. Bishop Duffy had also been instrumental in helping the sisters to obtain the desire of their hearts—status in the Church as religious. Here, too, were members of the old band ready to make their final vows—Sister Teresa and Sister Patricia, both of whom as young girls had been instructed by Miss Ellerker for their reception into the Church and who had been prepared for their First Communion by her.

They all felt the day chosen for the final vows a very significant one—Laetare Sunday. "Serve the Lord with gladness" had been their motto from the beginning when Father McNabb's talk had suggested it to them.

Bishop Duffy gave a very eloquent address, calling the sisters in a very true sense "ministers of the Lord," in their complete surrender of self and their life of prayer and union with God. Indirectly, too, he said, they were ministers of the Lord, in that they served Christ in the persons of the untaught, the poor, the sick and the aged.

Next day Mother Mary left to go to another group waiting for her, those at Duluth, which had been the first Corpus Christi House in the New World. It seemed very right that the day should be Corpus Christi day, for it carried them back to early days, back in fact to the time when Queenie Ellerker and her mother and sister arrived at the first little house in Leicester. Two of those three slept in the Lord now, but Mother Mary's other sister, Sister Mary Paul, was one of those who was making final vows at Duluth, as was Mother Mary Augustine, once a young sister here and now one of the Councillors.

Talking to them before the ceremony, Mother Mary told the community that she wanted them all to bear in mind the words of old Mère Geneviève to the little novice at Lisieux: "Serve the Lord in joy and peace, child. Remember always that Our God is a God of peace."

The feast day of the congregation was also the feast day of Mother Mary of the Blessed Sacrament. The sisters gathered about her in the afternoon to give her the gifts they had prepared for her. Together they recited the lovely prayer which had been written especially for them and which combined in a few words all their hopes and their endeavors, all the reason for their being religious of Mount Carmel.

"Our Lady of Mount Carmel and Cause of our Joy," they prayed, "send us generous souls who, under the guidance of the Holy Spirit, will be ever resourceful in working for the salvation of mankind. Give us your spirit of sacrifice, of humility and prayer. May we ever be characterized by our love for one another. Pray that we may love the Church and be permitted to serve it, its bishops and priests, for the salvation of souls.

"Saint Thérèse of the Child Jesus, pray for us."

When they had finished there was a moment's silence.

Then Mother Mary said, "Let us pray for one thing more, my dear daughters—for the fulfillment of that prayer."

There was one more ceremony to be performed in the midwest, that of the Scottsbluff sisters. They had finished the year's work on the Mexican missions and had now gone to Kearney for the summer to help there. So it was to Kearney that Mother Mary returned for the final vows of the one sister ready to make them. The Bishop of Grand Island, Bishop Bona, came to preside and he chose as his text, "Behold the handmaid of the Lord." Only later did he learn how apt had been his text, for those were the words which Sister Mercedes had chosen to be engraved on her ring.

That night, in her little room, Mother Mary saw on the wall a picture of Saint Thérèse, taken on the day she made her vows, and she remembered the young girl's words on that occasion and said them over as she looked out into the lovely late spring evening: "I felt that everything was little except the graces I had received and my peace and joy as I gazed at night on the lovely starlit sky."

A few days later Mother Mary was at Middletown, where the last of the ceremonies of final vows was to be carried out. This time a Carmelite, Father Flanagan, the New York provincial, presided. The little chapel was filled with Carmelite brothers from St. Albert's College and one of them played the organ. The sisters received the black veil and the ceremonies ended with a Te Deum, the prayer of praise which was a part of every profession ceremonial.

This time something very special emphasized the complete union with Christ which this ceremony carried out. When, after the prostration before the altar, the sisters rose to advance to the altar itself in the symbolic action which signified that Christ was now their Spouse, the Prior raised the cloth on the altar so that each sister might kiss the consecrated altar stone itself.

That day the group of sisters gathered about their Mother General to recite the litany of the Blessed Virgin, as they did each day. But when they repeated the special privileged invocations granted to Carmel, they spoke the words with a deeper understanding and love than ever before:

"Beauty of Carmel—Virgin Flower of Carmel—Patroness of Carmelites—Hope of all Carmelites—pray for us," they recited the beautiful words together and felt them deep in their minds and hearts.

# ELEVEN

By AUGUST OF 1932 MOTHER GENERAL HAD RETURNED TO Trinidad, where she planned to spend some months training the young sisters, a duty she loved. However, by spring of the next year, urgent business called her back to the States. She delayed her journey for some weeks at the advice of her doctor. She had had a severe attack of influenza which had weakened her heart; she also had an acute pain in her right hand which had not quite disappeared when she sailed on the *Eastern Prince*.

She reached Middletown in time to preside at the perpetual vows of Sister Carmelita and seemed to be getting better. But by April she was so ill that she had to remain in bed. Though she protested to the doctor that she would be quite well in a few days, he, to the alarm of the sisters, was by no means so optimistic. He said he thought the pain in her hand—now spreading into other joints—was the beginning of an arthritic condition which might well grow worse.

As soon as weather and the doctor permitted, she traveled to New York to consult a specialist who advised a dry climate for a time. This decided her to go to Duluth, partly because of the medical advice and partly because she was anxious to see the sisters in the northwest again.

Sister Teresa, who was her companion on this journey, across the States, had no easy task. Mother General grew steadily worse, and by the time they reached Duluth, she could scarcely walk. The sisters there were shocked at her condition, much more than was she. She wanted news of the houses and asked to see the newcomers whom she had not met. She did agree to treatments, and these, which continued for some months, resulted in improvement. For a time she had not been able to walk at all, but, after some months of treatment, she was able to take a few steps each day.

By the spring of 1934 it was decided that the best place for her was Trinidad. The heat there would be of more benefit to her than a merely dry climate, and the winters in Duluth were severe. Sister Mary Paul took her back to Port of Spain, but she could not stay to nurse her. The responsibility of the rural missions was hers and there was no one to replace her.

At the Motherhouse in Trinidad her sisters crowded to welcome her. When they saw her they all tried to conceal their grief at her appearance. She smiled at them as she was carried up the staircase to her room.

"I feel better already," she called reassuringly, and they

tried to smile back. But she was right. She did improve to some degree. The soft breezes from the hills and the tropic warmth were evidently what she needed.

Her community had exciting news for her about an event which had happened while she was away. The Dry River had definitely belied its name. After a heavy rain it had overflowed and had become a raging flood. Houses were swept away and others half filled with water.

The old people at the hospice were terrified and some of the sisters took them into the chapel and began reciting the rosary with them, while other sisters went to find out if they were in immediate danger at the hospice. They learned they would be safe and returned to reassure the old people. Despite the comforting words and the hot drinks, they still shivered with fright.

On the way home Sister Rita and Sister Mary had thought they heard voices across the road from where they were walking. It was deep in mud but they managed to get across and found five small children up to their waists in the mire. They brought them home, bathed them and put them to bed. Unlike the old people, these children had been in real danger but they looked on the whole thing as something of a lark.

Now the flood was past and Port of Spain was itself again. Mother General had come home just in time for the Corpus Christi procession and everyone was working to make it very fine. She insisted on helping with a beautiful canopy which the sisters were making. Her fingers were now too crippled with arthritis for her to do any of the embroidery but she made dozens of little tassels for the canopy and everyone was very proud of her handiwork.

On the feast day the procession marched over the grounds, following the chaplain who was carrying the Blessed Sacrament. The way led to the shrine of Our Lady, to an altar in the girls' playground and back to the chapel. Mother Mary could not join the procession but she watched it all from the gallery of the second floor of the Motherhouse.

By the feast of the Presentation she had so improved that one morning she gave her community a joyful surprise by walking to the chapel rail to receive Communion. Her improvement continued slowly, and by early in 1935 she was able to climb a short flight of steps.

Despite her illness she remained definitely at the helm of the ship. She carried out her office of Mother General. She was equally interested in the small stories of her communities in other places, and there was no lack of amusing incidents from the sisters who worked among the Mexican and on rural missions. Port of Spain, too, provided many incidents. Perhaps one of Mother Mary's favorites was the one which dealt with the adventurous evening of the community, sitting quietly in the refectory listening to spiritual reading and suddenly faced with jungle fact. Through the open door they saw the branches of a guava tree shaking violently, though there was no breeze to stir them. Suddenly a huge monkey appeared, obviously intending to come in the open door. The sisters left quietly but hurriedly.

One sister who had not been with the others heard quiet footsteps on the balcony and went out to investigate. She found herself face to face with the intruder, who was as surprised as she and leaped hastily back to his guava shelter. Eventually his owner came with a lasso and took him away. The sisters, freed of their unwelcome caller, breathed a prayer of gratitude. Mother Mary's reaction, when she heard about the encounter, was that she was very sorry she had missed it all.

In 1935 the island celebrated the silver anniversary of Archbishop Dowling. Since he was also ecclesiastical superior of their congregation, the Corpus Christi Sisters had their share in the ceremonies.

In the speech he made to the many people assembled to honor him, he thanked them all for having made it so wonderful an occasion, and he especially mentioned the Carmelite community. "I think the most important work I have done since I became archbishop," he said, "is to have brought the Corpus Christi sisters here in 1919. It is an honor to Trinidad and the Archbishop that they have their Motherhouse here. I think it is a unique honor and only fitting that they should help celebrate my silver anniversary this morning."

On Corpus Christi day in 1936 a new work was announced in Trinidad. A day nursery was set up on the grounds of the Girls' Industrial School. For years Dr. Laselle, the faithful doctor on the island, had had this dream of a place where young children could be cared for while their mothers were at work. He died before the day nursery became a reality, but it was his insistence which brought it into being. Everyone helped—store keepers, social workers, officials of the government. Toys were sent and furniture and offers came of financial help.

The home was to be open to all children of working mothers and they would be accepted within the ages of one month and three years. It was a fine example of love in action, an action to help those least able to help themselves. On the wall of the new nursery was hung a tablet in memory of Dr. Laselle and under it the small beneficiaries of his dream romped and slept.

In the United States, the work of the Corpus Christi sisters was progressing well. Duluth was extending its work, and at Scottsbluff the work among the Mexicans grew, too, though it was still to a great degree pioneer work. It was always work with excitement in it too. In other missions, life went peacefully enough but never in the Mexican mission. There the unexpected always happened.

The sisters found it easy to get women and children to come to Mass but much more difficult to persuade the men to come. One letter to Mother Mary boasted, "Five male Mexicans in church last Sunday." But faith was there. Once on a sick call the sisters found a little altar in the room where the sick woman lay, and under the crucifix was placed a little pile of coins—the family funds—and placed there for safety. "And safer than some of the banks in the west," commented Sister Josephine.

Once, called to a house, they found to their surprise not a Mexican family but a nice Irish family of blue-eyed boys and girls. The voluble grandmother who was bringing them up said she came to America seventy-three years before—"when Chicago was just a middling village."

On the way home, coming behind a haycart which suddenly dropped a pile of hay in the road, Sister Columba swerved to avoid it. Then, in Sister Josephine's account to Mother Mary, "the car sank gracefully in a ditch full of water. Raimondo, evidently embarrassed by the contretemps, refused to start again or rise. We had to telephone the garage to come and give him anything he could desire."

It was Sister Josephine who remembered and could relate the most touching of the stories of the Mexican mission. She knew well what the Faith meant to these people. She said one day that she had in her life seen many doors —on old castles, on ancient cathedrals, on homes large and small, but the door she remembered best was one of unpainted wood, crookedly hung and fastened with a decrepit latch. It was the entrance to a Mexican adobe hut.

It was ajar when she first saw it, though it was winter and the snow was deep around the little house. Paper flowers and tiny bells hung on it in welcome to the Guest who was coming. In the hut a young man lay dying. An old car drove up and from it alighted two Mexican boys, a priest, and Sister Josephine. All about the house stood relatives, waiting in the cold for this group to arrive. They all walked in procession behind the priest. At the entrance to the house were kneeling the women, their mantillas on their heads, holding tight their youngest to warm them from the bitter cold.

Inside the hut there had been an attempt at an altar made up of a small cheap statue on a box, and lighted candle ends. The sick man lay inert on the bed as the priest began the prayers for the dying. In the house and outside in the snow knelt the people, oblivious of everything except the man who was praying and the man whom he was helping to a good death.

During 1937 a novitiate was opened at Kearney. Now girls could be taken as postulants and trained in the United States. They would no longer need make the long and expensive journey to Trinidad.

There was, however, one incident in accomplishing this caused by the apprehensions of Mr. Keens when told of the plan. Would he, asked the sisters, have any objection if his former home was used as a novitiate. He looked startled at the question and asked, "But are you sure they will take care of the place? Won't they be wild girls?"

He was reassured. Mother Teresa assured him that most aspirants to the religious life were by nature quiet and docile girls. Mr. Keens then gave his consent, asking only that they continue to make their chief work at the Keens Home that of the care of the aged.

In that same year, a General Chapter was held in Trinidad. When the delegates from the United States arrived they were very anxious about Mother Mary whom they had not seen for several years. The previous news about her condition had been disturbing. Constant pain and consequent sleeplessness had affected her heart. On one occasion she had received the last Sacraments.

It was then, a pure delight and a great relief to see her, when they came up the steps of the Belmont Carmel, waiting to welcome them. She was so much better, they were told, that she was not even using her rolling crutch.

It was so good to see each other again, said the sisters. Letters had their place, but they were never so good as meeting face to face. There were many questions to ask and many things to be talked over. But what delighted the visitors most of all was to see that Mother Mary was still in complete charge of her congregation.

Everything was in gala array for the Chapter meeting. The chapel had been newly painted, the stalls revarnished. The nuns of St. Joseph had loaned to Belmont a wonderful chair of red velvet for the ceremonies. A new carpet made by the sisters had woven into it the Carmelite coat of arms. The altar, made of native cedar wood, was bright with crimson blooms; everywhere were other flowers and palms. Mass was to open the ceremonies. It was the feast day of Our Lady of Mount Carmel.

At nine o'clock Archbishop Dowling arrived with his vicar. The girls from the Industrial School were lined on the path from the gate to the main entrance of the house and there the prelates were met by Father O'Neill and representatives of various Orders: the Augustinian Father Bermejo, the Dominican Father Hilary and the Benedictine Prior of Mt. Saint Benedict. They entered the chapel while the sisters were singing. Then the Archbishop intoned the Veni Creator and the clergy joined him.

Archbishop Dowling was the speaker. In his sermon he reminded his hearers that this was a real occasion. "Once more we are making history," he said, "for never before in my episcopate nor in that of my predecessor or those before him has there been a general chapter held in this small island of Jamaica. It is small I admit, but it is not altogether inglorious, for it is dedicated to the Blessed Trinity."

It was now almost twenty years, he said, since he had first gone to meet the sisters in the harbor of Port of Spain. They had just come from England to take up work in the colony, and at his request. Now he was welcoming sisters of the same group once more, but this time not only from England but from various parts of the United States. He spoke of the years of work they had given to Trinidad, and he expressed his deep gratitude.

They would now, he said, proceed to the business at hand—the holding of elections. But first he wished to speak to the assembled sisters about the day on which these elections were being held, that of the feast day of Our Lady of Mount Carmel.

Carmel was not, considered as a mountain, very high, he said. "It rises from the slopes of Palestine and there is a very gradual slope to its summit. And so we must not ever be satisfied to remain where we are, in the low places, but gradually rise to higher perfection. Although we cannot actually reach the perfection of the angels and of the saints in Heaven in the manner of doing the will of God, yet we can approximate to this by supernaturalizing every moment both of day and night. As we read in the Canticle of Canticles: 'I sleep but my heart watches.'"

The result of the elections was that Mother Mary of the Blessed Sacrament was once more elected Mother General. Sister Teresa Johnson was re-elected as her first assistant. In addition eight superiors were elected, for the congregation had grown so that now it had that number of offices to fill—for the Industrial School, the Hospice for Aged, the Kearney Home, the Carmels at Duluth, Middletown and Scottsbluff. There were two novitiate mistresses to be chosen, for Trinidad and Kearney.

When the Archbishop had confirmed the elections, all went back to the chapel for Benediction of the Blessed Sacrament and the chanting of a Te Deum. It was sung with great fervor for they were all very happy and thank-

ful that they would have the one they called affectionately Little Mother with them again as General. It would,
in fact, have been difficult to think of anyone else as head
of the congregation than the one who had cared for it
since its beginning.

Before the visitors from the New World left for home,
they were taken to see the Industrial School and the day
nursery. In the latter place the prize exhibit was Amy
Violet, who had weighed four pounds when she was
brought to them, a sad little mite of six months and who
was now a healthy fourteen pounder with a big smile for
everyone and evidently in radiant health.

The visitors were also taken to some small missions
out in the country, a long drive through palm groves,
past sugar cane plantations, adobe huts, primitive oxcarts.
The women they passed wore pastel colored veils on their
heads and dozens of silver bracelets on their arms. Many
of the men whom they passed were clad in flowing white
robes and turbans; these were the pundits, the Hindu
priests.

The missions had as many nationalities as did the missions in Nebraska and Minnesota. Here were East Indians, Chinese, Malayans, Portuguese. Before the sisters
returned to the Motherhouse they went to call on an
orphanage in charge of French Dominican sisters. There
were only twenty sisters there for a family of over six
hundred. "But we do have wonderful lay helpers," said
the superior reassuringly, "and also mechanical helpers,"
and she showed the visitors the big electric mixers and the
great ovens which could bake twelve hundred loaves a
day and the shoemakers' shop which not only repaired

shoes but made new ones. They went to call also on the Sisters of St. Joseph to congratulate them on the recent celebration of their centenary of work on the island.

Last of all they visited their own shrine of Mount Carmel. This they did as part of a procession—cross bearer at the head, the laity with Our Lady's banner before them, the sisters. The boys' band from Belmont played as the procession wound along. At each station they all recited a decade of the rosary. Then the procession returned to the convent chapel where Benediction closed a day of Exposition.

Mother Mary had not been taken to the shrine. The grounds had been judged too damp. But she watched from the gallery of the Motherhouse as the procession left and she was still there to greet them when they returned.

On the next day the *Nerissa* took the delegates away, and those who watched them sail wondered what changes would come about before, in six years, they met again.

Early in the next year a gift came to Mother Mary and the Trinidad Carmel. It came from America and was a beautifully carved figure to be placed on the cross erected in the Motherhouse garden some years before. It was the loving work of one of the talented young sisters of the Duluth house.

On March 6 it was formally blessed by their chaplain, Father Fennesy, with altar boys, sisters, girls from the Industrial School, and visitors, marching through the house, singing a hymn in honor of the Passion. Then they all formed a semi-circle about the cross and its Figure.

It stood in background of rose bushes, swaying in the breeze as if in rhythm with the singing.

After the blessing each went to venerate the cross. Up in the gallery Mother General had watched it all and in spirit was at the foot of the cross with the rest. The ceremony ended with all present coming to the altar rail of the chapel to kiss the relic of the True Cross. And again Mother Mary in her wheel chair was part of the ceremony.

Mother Mary still tried to be of real help to the busy and often overworked sisters. Not long before, while staying at the hospice for a time, she replaced Mother Augustine, the superior, who had been sent to the United States to negotiate about a new home for the aged the congregation was hoping to open in Middletown. Despite her physical limitations, she had carried out all the duties of a local superior in Mother Augustine's absence.

Another task she made her own was that of distributing loaves of bread to the poor on several days a week. Very occasionally she went from the Motherhouse, as in May to St. Mary's College to take part in the Lourdes procession. There the Archbishop blessed, individually, over a hundred sick people, among them Mother General.

It was true that she was physically an invalid, and in many ways helpless, but her brilliant mind was as alert as ever. She was well able still to direct her congregation, even though she had to be carried up and down stairs for every function she attended. This was in itself an interesting sight. Six girls from the Industrial School carried her and it was considered a very high privilege to be one of her bearers.

Carefully and steadily the six girls carried Little Mother up and downstairs and to her various duties. They made a charming picture in their blue uniforms, their legs and feet brown and bare. And she lay quietly smiling, trusting them completely.

# TWELVE

IN 1938 ANOTHER PIECE OF WORK HAD BEEN UNDERTAKEN in Middletown, a Home for the Aged.

For some time there had been a search on for a suitable property for such a home; the sisters had been planning to open such a house for some years. Sometimes it seemed to them that one would never be found in the right neighborhood or at the right price. At last the many prayers had been answered.

They learned that a fine house was for sale on Highland Avenue and it was both within the city limits and the price asked was within their means. The New York provincial of the Carmelites came to look it over and approved highly. Mother Teresa was sent from Kearney to discuss matters with the owner. The city of Middletown voted a change in zoning so that the house could be used as a Home for the Aged.

Mother Augustine, the second assistant, then came from Trinidad to represent Mother Mary in signing the contract. The sisters were told they would be able to take possession in December when the owner would be leaving. They moved in three days after Christmas and the entire Carmel community in Middletown came to help celebrate the event. The Prior of the college blessed the house from basement to attic and last of all blessed the community kneeling before him in the great hall.

The other sisters returned to their convent, but two, Sister St. John and Sister St. Peter, remained in the new house with Mother Augustine and Sister Columba, to await the coming of their first old lady who was made comfortable in the room prepared for her.

Miss McLean was eighty-three years old. She had been born in Middletown and lived there all her life. Unable for some years to take care of herself, she had lived in a Protestant home where she had been well treated but where she felt the lack of what she wanted most: a Catholic chapel and Catholic surroundings. When she heard that a new home was being opened by Carmelite sisters, she immediately asked if she might come there.

She stood in the wide hall, looking about her, smiling and evidently very happy. "I am ready to go when God calls me," she told the sisters, "but I do hope He leaves me for a little while in this lovely place."

Next day a load of furniture came from the convent, followed by bedroom sets, wardrobes and a piano from friends. One room had been arranged as a chapel but for the first few weeks the two sisters in charge went to Mass at the nearest church. Then the Provincial secured from the chancery office permission for daily Mass and reservation of the Blessed Sacrament in their own home. The college loaned them all they needed for Mass and on January 28 the Prior himself said the first Mass and arranged that thereafter a priest would come daily to celebrate one.

A few months later the chapel received its own vessels, donated in the name of the mother of their good friends, the Nowns sisters. And during January the rest of the staff arrived, recruited from the houses in Duluth and Scottsbluff. Mother Mary Augustine was to remain in charge as prioress.

There was understandable surprise when word came that Mother Mary was planning to make a visitation of her American houses during 1940. No one had thought that she would ever do this again. The arthritic condition had made her more and more an invalid, more and more a prisoner in her own room. And now she was planning this long trip, arduous even for a person in the best of health.

However, when it was clear how much this meant to her, everyone began considering ways and means of making her as comfortable as possible for the long voyage. Her friends on the island insisted that she travel on as fast a boat as possible and a suite was taken for her on the *Argentine* which made the trip to New York in four and a half days. Mother Gertrude and Sister Mary Paul were to be her companions.

Though she was in pain much of the time, the sea voyage had not been too hard on her, Mother Gertrude wrote to her worried community in Trinidad. When they reached New York they were met at the dock by Mother Augustine and Sister St. Peter, who told them that Mother Angeline Teresa, Mother General of the Carmelite sisters in the Bronx, had offered them hospitality. When, however, she learned that it had been thought best that Mother Mary be taken immediately to Middletown, she had offered the car belonging to her own community, and a driver. Through her kindness, the travelers were taken the entire seventy miles to St. Teresa's Guest House. Mother Mary, thanks to this thoughtful gesture, made an excellent trip and could not express her thanks enough.

She was very tired, however, and was taken to her room to rest while Mother Gertrude told the community about the trip. Only one thing had marred it and that was the death of Archbishop Dowling only a few days before they left. He had been found dead in his chair, the morning paper still in his hands. With his going the community had lost a great friend, as indeed had all Trinidad. The city flags were flown at half mast in his honor.

It was comforting to know that in his place would be Dr. Finbar Ryan, appointed coadjutor three years before, another good friend of the community. He was among those who, when, as Dominican tertiaries, they were asking for canonical approval from Rome, had written his support of their petition and had grieved when it was not granted.

At Middletown an anxious group of sisters had been much relieved when they had seen Mother Mary's wide smile and heard her voice, vibrant as of old. But it was evident to those who had seen her three years before in

Trinidad that her condition was worse. It was also clear that, despite her crippled condition, she was in good spirits and ready to enjoy her visit.

A few days after her arrival Father Doswald, Prior General of the Carmelites, on visitation from Rome, came to call with his young English speaking assistant, Father Pausback. On the feast of Our Lady of Mount Carmel Father Flanagan, the provincial, sang the Mass in the little chapel and later presided when the community proceeded to the election of local superiors. These, according to the rule, took place every three years.

On the following day Mother Mary and her companions left for New York to begin the thirty-hour trip to Duluth by train. The fifteen hundred miles proved a real endurance test and trial, not only for the invalid but for her anxious companions. The train went so fast that Mother General had at times to be held in her berth so that she would not be thrown out. Then, too, there were several changes of trains and this meant that the windows of the Pullman had to be removed so that her stretcher could be taken through them, for the aisles were too narrow. Once, however, she was strapped to the stretcher and carried upright through a narrow doorway.

Mother General tried to be as helpful as possible with the train attendants. The sisters noted too how gently the men handled her; several times there were tears in their eyes as she was taken from train to train. They tried always to answer her pleasant smile with one of their own.

On July 20th, they reached the house at Duluth in an ambulance. The community was waiting at the door, anxious for a first sight of their beloved visitor. Those who had not seen her for some years found it difficult to hide their concern from her, so saddened were they by the change in her condition.

They all concealed as well as they could their apprehension from her for she was obviously so happy to be with them that she seemed to have forgotten she was an invalid. She asked many questions and they answered, happy that their news was good. Things were going well in Duluth. They were no longer going to be dependent on alms alone for much of their work, for the Duluth Community Fund was giving them a share from the big drive made once a year.

Even before she left Trinidad Mother Mary had planned her entire series of visitations and exactly how they were to be carried out. She wanted to celebrate a feast of Our Lady at each Carmel she visited, if that were possible. So, on the eve of the Assumption, and with a thunderstorm raging, she left the Duluth Carmel on her stretcher and began by way of a night train the thirty hour journey to Nebraska and Kearney. With her went Mother Gertrude and another sister who was returning to that Carmel.

Mother Mary was unperturbed by wind or rain or about the hard train trip either. She was reminiscing about the time twenty years before when Sister Teresa and Sister Mercedes and she had come for the first time to Duluth and had seen their home on the sky line, and of the friendly welcome given them by the Hilltop Workers.

They crossed Iowa by day but when they reached Nebraska it was dark night, with a great yellow harvest moon riding high in the heavens. They reached Kearney at two in the morning and found that Mr. Anderson, who functioned as undertaker and who had been told of Mother Mary's helpless condition had brought the only conveyance which would take care of her—his undertaker's ambulance. In this she was placed and the car went slowly and carefully into the prairie night. Moonlight silvered the trees and hedges as an early dawn began to lighten the sky.

Mother Mary was put to bed in the room prepared for her. When she woke later in the morning, it was to the sound of music: the novices and postulants were singing the "Gaudens Gaudebo," the introit of the Mass of Our Lady of Mount Carmel. It made a touching greeting for their Mother who had traveled almost five thousand miles to see them and become acquainted with them. The Scottsbluff sisters were there too, having come to Kearney so that Mother Mary would not have to make that long journey.

She listened with deep interest to the stories they told her of the missions and laughed heartily at Mr. Keens' fear of the "wild postulants." She loved the story of the clover blossom wreaths which the sisters had made for a First Communion class of Mexican girls and agreed they must have looked lovely.

She had a lovely story of her own to tell them, something which had happened only a few months ago and which concerned a small group of religious with whom those who had lived in Trinidad were familiar. For many years this small community, called Little Sisters of Charity of St. Dominic, had done wonderful work among the poor of the island. With time the numbers dwindled until there were left only the superior, one choir nun and one lay sister. Mother Madeleine died and Sister Teresa of the

Child Jesus and the lay sister were left alone. When the Dominicans offered the lay sister shelter, Sister Teresa came to Mother Mary with a request: would she accept her as one of her daughters?

The Archbishop had approved. "And so she came to us," said Mother Mary. "Even in these few months she has proved as generous a worker as a Carmelite as she was as a Dominican. What made her happiest of all was that she was able to keep her name. How could we call her anything else when she came to us with that name?"

The next week was a busy one. Bishop Bona of Grand Rapid Island, their ordinary, came to call and to discuss matters with Mother Mary. She was driven to the town of Kearney and taken to the cemetery where some of her daughters were buried and she prayed over them. One evening the novices gave a play in her honor and she enjoyed it very much.

She had been two weeks in Kearney when word came that Sister St. Peter, prioress of one of the Middletown Carmels, had had a stroke and was not expected to live. Mother Mary decided to shorten her visit and go back there at once.

She had to break her journey at Chicago because there were no through trains. Knowing this and that she had several hours to wait between trains, she had written to an arthritis specialist, who offered to come to the station to see her. From this unusual sort of doctor's call came suggestions on her disease which later proved very helpful. His advice helped to make her movements less restricted and she was able to write with her pen held between two fingers of her right hand.

But that was in the future. Now the trip back proved

as difficult as had been the one which brought her to the northwest. In Middletown they found Sister St. Peter still very ill and Mother Mary had her taken to the Guest House by ambulance so that she could be closer to her. She also decided to delay her own return for a time, but when Sister St. Peter's condition remained unchanged and the doctor said she was in no immediate danger, Mother Mary decided to go back to Trinidad.

It was no easy matter to secure a sailing. The second world war was in its first phases and it was next to impossible to find a place for three civilians. Eventually they sailed on a freighter, the only vessel available. They were the only women on board and were given the officers' berths. Everyone was very kind to the invalid and the sisters were very grateful.

The *Arabian Prince* was not a fast ship, as had been the one which brought them to New York. It took twelve days to make the journey. It was a hard trip, not only because of the slowness of the ship but because of the nightly blackouts. But the invalid never lost her cheerfulness though it was clear to her companions that she was often in great pain.

Chiefly she spoke of her happiness at having made one more trip to the United States, the country she loved and of which she had been a citizen for some years. "I am an American citizen," she would tell people with a twinkle in her eye. "I am British by birth and American by choice."

On the eve of the feast day of St. Thérèse the long hard journey at last ended. She had covered ten thousand miles by ship, train, and car. The *Arabian Prince* made a special stop in the harbor at Port of Spain in order to land the three religious. The officers carried Mother Mary carefully down to the launch, and at the customs they were met by a group of sisters and some old friends, among them Dr. Carrington, who had known her for thirty years.

Next day the Carmel at Trinidad celebrated the feast day with great joy as well as with great relief. There had been continuous worry about this long and arduous visitation, yet no one had opposed it, not even her doctors. They all knew it had been the desire of her heart, due to a strong sense of duty as well as motherly instinct, to make this last visitation of her American houses, to greet the sisters whom she knew, to talk with the new members who had never known her. The community, which had been waiting daily for untoward news, settled down again to its usual routine. Mother was at home again. She had survived the long voyage, the trips from train to train, from ship to ship, and her own happiness at her accomplishment was cause enough for them to be happy that she had completed it successfully.

To the houses in the United States went immediate word of the safe return, and letters from those foundations told how happy they had been to have had, even briefly, their beloved Mother with them. They were fortified for the work by her joy in their successes. They had been given strength by seeing her, so crippled, so ill, yet able to be of help to them by her very presence.

During the year before her visitation and the years immediately following had come word of the death of several friends of long ago, who had worked with Queenie Ellerker in her first years at Leicester. Anne

McDiarmid who had given her talents and her funds to the work during her years with the Corpus Christi group, died at the Dominican convent at Stone, England where she had spent the rest of her long life as a lay tertiary.

Their other early co-worker, Emily Fortey, was still at work, though growing old now in service. Over the years she had established nursery homes for working mothers and cared for unmarried mothers and their babies in the homes which she had built to shelter them. Her friend Mabel Tothill, a Quaker, said, "She makes no noise; she just gets things done," and Mother Mary said that was a perfect definition of her. She had been much amused to learn that at the age of seventy Emily had decided she must learn to swim. She had always been very afraid of the water and felt she must overcome this.

"I don't mind one clear call for me and I wouldn't be afraid to answer it. But I do a little dread a lingering illness." When she died she was buried from Holy Cross Church where years ago had stood the Corpus Christi House where Sister Emily Catherine had lived and worked.

Another friend of years was gone—Miss Eliza Murphy. A few years after her furniture arrived at Middletown, she came also, too tired by that time to sleep or even to rest. She was still an uncertain Catholic when she came and felt, as she expressed it, cold to the Faith. But one morning she told the sisters in great excitement that a strange thing had happened to her.

"I thought I was asleep and had all but dropped off. I thought I heard a soft voice say, 'There is someone downstairs who would like to see you.'"

"I'll be right down," she had answered promptly, and

then, by that time wide awake, she realized it was the middle of the night and no one would be calling her. As suddenly she knew who "someone" was: it was Our Lord in the chapel and the one who had come to summon her was little Saint Thérèse for whom, even when she felt no love for the faith itself, she had had great devotion ever since she read the life of her which Mother Mary had sent her. After that message she gave up her hesitation and her fear and became what she had always been in spirit, a true and practicing Catholic.

During her years in Middletown she had been a great benefactor of the community. They would miss her for all her kindnesses to them. But more than the material aid, they would miss her for that period of spiritual rebirth.

In 1943 came another death, this time that of the man who had bound them so closely together in their beginning—Father Vincent McNabb. When, two years before, he had celebrated his golden jubilee in London at St. Dominic's Priory, Mother Mary sent him a congratulatory letter and he wrote back promptly. It was said by those who knew him best that Father McNabb treasured everything anyone had ever done for him, and this letter showed it.

"Among the treasured memories of my half century of priestly life, few are so treasured as the sisterly help you gave me for six years. I am not good at giving thanks either by word or deed, but I think I have a remembering heart. Pray for me."

The Corpus Christi annals of early days said of him, "He was for six years the soul of a body which without him would have died a speedy death." The difference in the wording of his letter and the statement in the annals was the measure of the priest who had been their friend.

Only a few of the community were left who remembered those early days when the priest who was famous all over London for his sermons, who held thousands enthralled in Hyde Park, gave hours of his time to talk to the group of young women at New Walk, and when a young Queenie Ellerker copied in a neat script all that he was saying to them. Always he was the humble Dominican friar, a beggar as he called himself, encouraging the young women before him, blessing the work they were doing—"an epic of Catholic Action" he called it. And, when they became members of Mount Carmel, his was one of the first messages blessing their future work.

He had encouraged them in their first work for souls, that of the reunion of Christendom, for which purpose they had been founded. They often remembered, years later, little phrases of his when they were in doubt or difficulty: "Take good where you find it"— "See that you always understand the other person's point of view."— "Acknowledge truth wherever it is found"— "Don't prove some other religion is false; be positive about your own."

In the Corpus Christi Chronicle, the little magazine which the Kearney community had been publishing for years, Mother Mary wrote all this about him as a memorial to him. "To him we owe our first training in the religious life," she wrote, "a training so complete and so careful that when God's time came for us to receive canonical erection as a congregation of Carmelites, there was very little new for us to learn and we had nothing to unlearn. His own life was our greatest, simplest and most persuasive lesson. To look at him, to watch him, was to learn how to pray and how to work."

Among her papers Mother Mary found a bit of verse he had sent her, a farewell letter when he left the Leicester priory and was sent to the one near London. She asked that it be read to the community. It was written on a creased half sheet of note paper, for he was apt to utilize any scrap of paper to write on:

*"Of thanks a little meed*
*For a great unthanked deed.*
*A beggar man's return*
*For kind gifts that burn.*
*A priest's sole way*
*Of saying his own say,*
*And saying it with prayer*
*That Heaven may be an air*
*To enfold you everywhere."*

Of his many letters she chose one to have read to the community, one on the Real Presence. "There is a sense in which Our Lord's apostolic work began only with the first Mass celebrated by Saint Peter," he wrote. "Since then, though not everyone sees it, His apostolic life in the Blessed Sacrament is beyond fathoming . . . Wherever He is, He is the Priest of the Parish. Not only does He dwell on the altar, but from the altar He pours forth into the souls of the parish all the riches of His love and grace. May you never give up your desire to copy Him in His altar apostolate."

# THIRTEEN

IN 1946 A PETITION WAS PRESENTED AT ROME ASKING FOR papal approval of the Corpus Christi congregation and its constitutions. There were, of course, many things militating against granting the Decree of Praise at that time. The members were still few, the foundations small. To their great joy Mother Mary received the paper for which they had prayed so heartily. With it came a copy of the revised constitutions which they were now to follow.

Towards securing this, Archbishop Ryan had been especially influential. He had been in Rome at the time it was presented and, knowing the Holy Father's deep interest in missionary work and native vocations, he had stressed the fact that this congregation was a pioneer in the work of training local colored girls in Trinidad, and that they now had over fifty members in their congregation who worked among their own people of the Caribbean.

Others had been of great help, especially the Carmelite heads in Rome, Cardinal Spellman and the bishops in whose dioceses they had houses; all had written letters of recommendation. The assistant general of the Carmelites, Father Pausback, who had some years before helped the sisters with their rescript, was delighted with this proof of their advance.

"Only when we get to Heaven," he wrote to Mother Mary, "shall we know whom to thank for the marvellous speed with which this had gone through." And Mother Mary wrote in return that she knew one great help had been the prayers offered at Lisieux, where the nuns had been praying hard for their missionary sisters' success.

Some time before, an old timer arrived in Trinidad, coming from Kearney in time to take part in the celebration of the silver anniversary of the Corpus Christi Sisters first foreign mission house. Sister Josephine had been one of the first members in Trinidad in 1919; she had worked there for almost fifteen years and she felt much at home, happy to be back even though most of the old people she had once cared for were long gone. One whom she remembered well had just died, at the age of eighty-four.

"Lily Este was a great help to us in the early days," she said reminiscently. "I remember how often she saved us from being imposed on by unscrupulous salesmen."

Despite her old affection for Trinidad it was clear that the missions of the United States also held her heart.

She entertained the sisters with tales of her mission classes there, of the many nationalities she taught—Italian, Greek, Mexican, German. "Many of the children had never seen a nun," she said, "and were afraid of us at first because they thought we were some kind of ghost. But they got over that soon. They are such good eager little children. They are a joy to work with."

Long ago, when she came to Miss Ellerker in Leicester, the doctor who examined her had agreed with her that she was not very strong. But for thirty years she had carried on, and usually in her own inimitable fashion. She had one formula for the sores with which so many in Trinidad were afflicted. The wound was washed well. Lourdes water was poured on it and the patient was told to say a Hail Mary; if she could not, Sister Josephine said it. Clean bandages were put on and the patient was given a piece of bread and jam and sent home.

She was tired and ill when she came back to Trinidad; it was hoped that the warm climate would benefit her. But she died several years after she returned to her first mission home. The tired frame had at last refused to follow the commands of the indomitable spirit. Only a week before her death she came to Mother Mary's office, radiantly happy because after long effort she had tracked down a family and had their promise that the children would be sent for instruction. Not until the last few days of her life did anyone except herself know that she was suffering from cancer.

During those years of war much of the work of the sisters, as well as that of everyone else, was more or less disrupted. Sisters in every country had been affected, and in every Corpus Christi House the sisters were praying for the safety of religious everywhere.

One day Mother Mary, reading an English newspaper, found an account of prisoners of war, and there was mention of a group of nuns who had been interned at Vittel. They were of many nationalities and they had elected one of their number to act as superior for them all. Her name was Mother Agnes Stuart, of the Little Sisters of the Poor. "And that," said Mother Mary, looking at her community as she put the paper down, "is our own Agnes Stuart who was one of the first Children of Mary at Leicester."

The story told how the religious were all interned in a hotel; they turned half of it into a convent and the other half into a shelter for two hundred old men who had no place to live. Then the three hundred nuns of many different orders had elected Mother Agnes to set up a school for the more than a hundred children in the camp and had organized a collective kitchen which combined the camp fare and Red Cross parcels. When the camp's dwellers were repatriated, she and some of the other sisters stayed on to care for the British prisoners still held there.

"It says that she talked back when she had to go to the Nazi commanders, and I have no doubt she did," said Mother Mary with delight. "Evidently she is the same energetic Agnes we knew in the old days."

In the spring of 1947 was held the third General Chapter, postponed from 1943 because of the war. It took place at the Belmont Carmel in Trinidad.

Mother Teresa was already there. Mother Gertrude came from some months spent in England to take a refresher course in social work. Many of those who came as delegates had not seen each other for at least seven years. It was a joyous reunion.

At this General Chapter local prioresses were to be elected for nine houses—four in Trinidad, two in Nebraska, one in each for Minnesota, New York, and Pennsylvania. Their work now included a great variety—catechetical teaching, care of the aged, parish visiting, probation work, care of delinquent girls, day nurseries, retreat work.

Archbishop Ryan presided at the election and afterwards spoke to the assembled members. "You are now not merely a diocesan institute," he told them, "but a pontifical congregation. You have received the Decree of Praise and the approval of your constitutions and this marks the beginning of a new and important phase of your existence."

Mother Mary of the Blessed Sacrament was again elected as Mother General. As the *Chronicle* expressed it, "Since she is the foundress of the congregation, it seems only fitting that she should remain in that office as long as God gives her the strength to do so."

Many new foundations had been opened since the sisters had last come together and each group told the story of her own.

In Trinidad a new foundation had been made in 1945, at Tunapuna, a town some ten miles from Port of Spain. The arrival of the sisters who were to live there had been made a matter of real celebration. They came by car and when they reached the town they were met by a whole procession—cross bearer, acolytes, priests, and back of them what looked like the whole parish—small boys and girls in First Communion dress, laywomen, and Holy Name Society. The papal colors were everywhere.

Everyone crowded into the church which was soon filled to overflowing. There were prayers and hymns, and then the sisters were taken to their convent by another procession, a smaller one, at its head Dr. Meenan of St. Mary's College, who blessed the rooms. Then they all returned to the church for a High Mass where the children sang the Mass of the Angels and Dr. Meenan spoke to the congregation on the text: "I announce to you a great joy." He gave a short exposition of Carmelite history, spoke of the special group who had come to work at Tunapuna, and then turned to the five sisters in the front pew. "And now," he said impressively, "in the language of my own country, a hundred thousand welcomes to you."

Also opened in Trinidad, two years before, was the convalescent home for children, now flourishing. It was the first such home on the island and it was open to all children, regardless of creed or color. The social welfare worker in the city had come to Mother Mary about this great need; the overcrowded hospitals, she explained, could not keep the children, yet to send them to their homes often meant complete lack of care and renewed illness.

At the time, the sisters were rather in the position of Saint Peter: silver and gold they had none, but they could offer their hands and hearts and they did. In response to their appeal, a public subscription was opened and nearly half the necessary funds had been collected when it opened. When it was dedicated, the Archbishop formally dedicated the building and the Governor of the island was a guest.

One of the delegates to the Chapter, Mother Teresa Mary, had much to tell of the new little mission house in Johnstown, Pennsylvania, of which she was superior.

It had been opened at almost the moment the war ended; in fact, the train, in which the sisters who were to make the foundation were riding, reached the city at the exact time when word of the war's end had come. As they alighted from the train they were greeted by the noise of whistles and sirens and shouts that heralded the longed for peace. It was so nicely timed that they all but felt the demonstration had been for them.

When they reached their new home in the Italian parish of St. Anthony, they found that despite the excitement about peace there had been no lack of preparation for the newcomers. The kitchen shelves were filled with canned goods, with soap and preserves. Waiting for them was a delicious Italian dinner.

It was obvious that the whole convent had been done over and it was well furnished. The senior sodality of the parish had a special party in their honor. Even the ice cream welcomed them, and very literally, for the word appeared in pink letters on each slice.

In the evening, after the party, they joined the parishioners in the church to give thanks for peace. Novenas were begun, to Saint Anthony and Saint Rocca and, to the delight of the Carmelites, to Saint Thérèse. Peace had come on a wonderful day—on the great feast of the Assumption.

Now the sisters were teaching—nearly three hundred

children in their classes—and they were beginning parish visiting. They were very busy and very happy.

Middletown too reported continuous growth. By that year of 1947 there were eighteen sisters in that city. The Home for the Aged was filled and the house next door had been acquired. They were now planning to turn the large garage at the rear of their property into a retreat house for laywomen. The Carmelite Fathers had thought it would be a good idea to invite groups of girls from New York and other cities for week end retreats. They too thought it a fine idea but they had been too crowded to dare consider it. This would give them the opportunity.

Mother Gertrude, while she was in England, had attended a meeting of social welfare workers in London and had been delighted, she told the delegates, when one official from New York rose to speak of Saint Teresa's Guest House in Middletown as "second to none in the east." She had been treasuring the compliment until she could bring it to the Middletown delegates.

A year later, when the plan regarding the garage was completed, the sisters at Middletown wrote Mother Mary that no one would ever recognize the old garage. St. Joseph's Retreat House, which was its name, had twenty-three rooms, in addition to a large sitting room. The walls were painted a warm cream color; there were pretty drapes, plenty of pictures, comfortable furniture. The new project was fulfilling a need, for the rooms were filled at each retreat.

They were already planning a further development of the retreat idea: to hold Cana retreats, where couples could come for week ends with their children, whom the sisters would care for while their parents could give themselves completely to the retreat.

The first one, held during 1948, proved an interesting and novel affair. The children were taken in charge by the sisters. In the yard were swings and slides; in the house were stories and naps and good meals for them. Meantime the grownups were free to give all their time to discussion periods, which were also held during the evening over coffee and cigarettes. There was a daily Mass and during the day short talks on both the spiritual and the practical sides of marriage, the things which injured it; the things which made it work better. Late Sunday afternoon the retreat ended after the eight couples who had come had renewed their marriage vows in the chapel. Then each couple collected its children and departed after loudly praising their week end.

Father Dowling, the Jesuit who had been retreat master, said the retreat had been history making. "This is the first convent to accept such a family group," he said. "Like all great things it is starting small, But, then, the Church started in a small way too."

# FOURTEEN

THE RAVAGES OF THE DISEASE WHICH HAD CRIPPLED
Mother Mary over the years made greater and deeper in-
roads. The poor fingers were terribly twisted and bent and
she was often in pain. But her spirit was unquenched. Her
eyes still lighted with interest at what her sisters came to
tell her they were doing, or at the contents of the letters
which came to her from the various Carmels.

She now had her room and her office on the main floor
because she was increasingly helpless. She was not happy
to be so far away from the chapel but the sisters liked
the change for it meant they saw more of her.

In August of 1948 she had sent a circular letter to all
her houses. "Getting old," she wrote, "means getting un-

adaptable, getting set in your ways, and a Corpus Christi Carmelite should never grow old. We should pray with Michael Field:

> "*Let me come to Thee young,*
> *When Thou dost challenge, 'Come.'*
> *With all my marvellous dreams unsung,*
> *Their promise by first passion stung,*
> *Though chary, dumb—*
>
> *Thou callest, 'Come!'*
> *Let me rush to Thee when I pass,*
> *Keen as a child across the grass."*

Each morning at Mass we call on God to renew the joy of our youth. It seems to me that one of the ways God has of preventing our becoming old is just this change in our life and conduct which passing from one superior to another entails. It keeps our minds and wills supple . . . Let each one strive to make her convent a house of joy in which everyone is happy."

At the end of the letter she quoted the remark of a former superior general of the Little Sisters of the Assumption: "Sow joy in souls if you wish to see them grow in virtue. Before wishing to sanctify those dear to you, first make them happy. Nothing so prepares a soul for God's grace as the happiness we procure for it." And her sisters, as they heard read the words which Mother Mary had quoted from another general, thought how well they applied to their own Mother.

During the latter part of the year she grew worse and by December she was close to death. Her Christmas letter was written for her and sent out by Mother Gertrude.

To those who had written her that they regretted any sorrow they had caused her in the past, she sent word: "Tell them their Little Mother will carry to God only an account of their loyalty and devotion." And she asked that their chief characteristic be always their love for each other.

In her letter to the houses Mother Gertrude wrote that Archbishop Ryan had come many times during the past two months to see the invalid. She gave other details of the various works of the congregation, but at the end she returned to the subject of their Mother General who had asked her to send each daughter her blessing. Mother Gertrude said she wished that she could enclose in each letter the smile of motherly love with which Mother General had spoken these words.

It was the custom of the community at Belmont to keep a reunion of the houses in the West Indies each year. It was impossible for all the members of the Trinidad houses to come together for Christmas, so they chose the feast which came three days later, that of Saint John the Evangelist.

Fifty sisters sat down together in the refectory at lunch time. Only two seats were empty—that of Little Mother, who they all felt was really there with them, and that of Sister Mary Paul who stayed with her in her room. Several others were missing who had been with them the year before, Sister Josephine and Sister Teresa Brigid. In the prayers after grace there was a special memento for them.

Just as they were beginning to eat, Sister Mary Paul came into the refectory with a slip of paper. It was a message for the New Year from Reverend Mother, she explained, and Mother Gertrude read it aloud. It was very brief.

"My dear little children," she read, "love one another. The mischief maker is detestable in the sight of God and man. Avoid any word, action or the repeating of things heard which could be a cause of pain, ill feeling, or strife among our sisters. Your Little Mother."

She had also sent down a printed breviary marker once given her and which had verses on it of which she was very fond. They were part of a long poem by Jean Ingelow and were called *Welcome Joy:*

> *"Take home Joy and make a place*
> *In thy great heart for her,*
> *And give her time to grow and cherish her;*
> *Then will she come and oft will sing to thee*
> *When thou art working in the furrow;*
> *Ay, or weeding in the sacred hour of dawn.*
>
> *It is a comely fashion to be glad—*
> *Joy is the grace we say to God."*

During the days which followed, the sisters at the Motherhouse realized to the full the statement which Father McNabb had made years before when he gave a talk on serving Christ personally through the sick, that a house with a sick subject who knew how to suffer was the next best thing to having the Blessed Sacrament there. It was indeed true of their Carmel and of the sick subject whose life was coming to an end there.

On January 7 of 1949 she was in such pain that her face reflected it, as did the groans she could not always suppress. She was given a sedative to control the pain, but it was evident that the drug did not in the least cloud her mind. When on January 10th the Archbishop came and stood beside her bed, she looked up at him and made an attempt to smile. Then she managed to hold his hands within her own poor twisted ones, and said in a low voice, "I am sorry for my sins." He blessed her. And so her last blessing of all was given her by a Dominican prelate.

On the morning of the 11th, when Sister Teresa Wine-frede was standing beside her bed, the dying woman reached up and caught sister's rosary in her fingers and held it, at the same time speaking with great difficulty a single word, "Jesus." Then suddenly her face seemed to alter. The doctor who had just left was recalled. A few moments after he came back into the sick room, Mother Mary of the Blessed Sacrament died.

Just before her death her face had been twisted in agony and it looked furrowed and lined, not only with pain but with the weight of her seventy-four years. She looked very small and frail as she lay there. Yet, a few hours later, when she was taken to the chapel, her whole appearance had changed. The lines of pain and the lines the years had made were gone. The small hands were smooth, too, not wrinkled as they had been. When she lay in her coffin she looked less than fifty years old. The sisters who remembered thought she looked exactly as she had when Miss Murphy took a picture of her many years before, in her white habit.

Five of the young sisters who were to renew their vows that day did this kneeling beside her body. They kissed her ring, the ring on which had been engraved the motto in Greek which Father McNabb had given her and which she had observed all through her life—"Generous with God."

Later, when the Office of the Dead was said, it seemed to her sisters a little strange to say a Magnificat, that prayer of joy. But it was very right too, they knew: she seemed still very near them, as she had promised to be.

She had left a letter asking that no more be said about her than was said about any sister. But she had not been dead two hours when the sisters were asked to broadcast word of her death. By noon the whole island knew that "Little Mother"—the only name they called her—was dead. There was to be a low early Mass at the convent chapel and later a solemn requiem Mass at Holy Rosary Church, the church she had so dearly loved.

The coffin was brought to the sanctuary. It was opened and the sisters were able to look again on their Mother's face and kiss her once more. It was found necessary to leave the coffin open after the Mass, for people crowded up to look at her. There were so many that the priests had to regulate the number of those who wanted to go past the coffin and touch their rosaries to her hands—men and women and children who had known and loved her for years, coming to take a last look at the peaceful beautiful face.

After the Mass was over, Archbishop Ryan spoke movingly of the faith and the life of good works and the virtues of Mother Mary of the Blessed Sacrament. He spoke of the great help she had been to the archdiocese, even in her later days of illness. "We must pray," he ended, "that if she is not already in Heaven she may speedily reach the reward she undoubtedly merited by her life of sacrifice and suffering of years."

At the cemetery the funeral cortège, the Archbishop, the sisters and many friends were met by the Abbot and the Benedictine monks who sang the "Benedictus." Then the Archbishop recited the last prayers.

Before the coffin was lowered into the ground two young Indian girls from Tunapuna laid a white cloth trimmed and sewed with ferns and white flowers into the grave.

As they had been a part of her all her long life, so now there were various Orders present in the ceremonies at her death. She had begun her religious life with Dominicans and it was they who sang her last Mass, while a Dominican archbishop spoke from the pulpit about her holy life and said the last blessing at her grave. Carmelites were all about her. She was buried in the cemetery of the Benedictines where some of her daughters already lay. It was a quiet lovely place where the noises of the city were muted. Close by the hill top which was God's acre, monks would chant the Office she had so loved. She was at peace there with the holy dead.

Hundreds came to the convent during the next days to ask for a "relic." One seminarian asked for Little Mother's spectacles, for he was certain that this was one thing he might have since no one else could use them. But not only the religious or the people she had worked with spoke of how they would miss her. From Governor's House came a message from Governor Shaw, offering the community his deep sympathy for their loss. "Mother Mary Ellerker selflessly performed for many years devoted and valuable work here. She was much loved and respected by all who knew her," he wrote.

Father Theodore Bull, prior of Holy Cross at Leicester,

wrote that it was a joy to remember how great a part Dominicans had played in her life, even to the very end. Father O'Sullivan, parish priest of St. Xavier's Church in Port of Spain, wrote of "our grand Little Mother" and hoped she would in Heaven remember the congregation and all who had loved and admired her on earth.

From Lisieux came a letter from the Carmel there. "We need not tell you the immense part we take in your sorrow," they wrote, and said the congregation must take courage from the fact that from eternity she was watching over her children.

From Dora Ibbertson, welfare head in the West Indies, and not a Catholic, came a letter of sorrow at their loss and hers. "She was a woman of such invincible goodness and warmth that to know her was to love her and she must have made Trinidad a better place for many others as she did for me," she wrote.

Some weeks after Mother Mary's death children from the Industrial School went to bathe in Manzanilla Bay. They brought home with them buckets of cockle shells.

"Let's put them around Mother's grave," one suggested and with Sister's permission they climbed the hillside, reciting the rosary as they toiled up the hill. They arranged about her grave a lovely design of colored shells. It was a charming offering to one who had always had a special love for the children of Trinidad.

## FIFTEEN

WHEN MOTHER MARY OF THE BLESSED SACRAMENT WAS dying, she had asked that at her death the Mother Assistant take her stall in the chapel. Therefore Mother Gertrude took over the duties and affairs of the congregation until, at a General Chapter held in Trinidad in May of 1941 Mother Teresa Johnson was elected superior general. She had, many years before, been one of the young girls whom Miss Ellerker had instructed in the Faith at Leicester. She had known the foundress since she was a girl of fourteen. In fact, she and her sister Gertrude and Mother Mercedes Chapman had been three of the group of Children of Mary who had become Corpus Christi Sisters.

Early in the spring of 1950 occurred at Trinidad something of which Mother Mary would have loved to be a part. The pilgrim statue of Our Lady of Fatima, in the course of its long travels, came to Trinidad, and was welcomed by the Corpus Christi Sisters in each of their four convents on the island.

Great preparations had been made. The statue arrived in the special car, deep blue in color with *Ave Maria* in gold letters on its sides, in which it traveled. In the procession in Our Lady's honor the Corpus Christi Sisters marched directly behind the car. The statue remained one night in the convent at Diego Martin and there a shrine had been prepared to receive it. The sisters took turns praying there all through the night.

Another event, this time in England, would also have rejoiced Mother Mary's heart. In October the White Friars made an official return to the ancient Carmelite friary at Aylesford where, over four hundred years before, the community had been driven out during the suppression of the monasteries. It was a holy place for the Order, for it was the town where Saint Simon Stock had built the first house in England and where, five years after its foundation in 1245, the first General Chapter of the Carmelite Order was held, at which Saint Simon Stock was elected prior general.

The church had been long ago destroyed but the foundation stones had been uncovered. The church and the monastery were to be restored so that the friars would be once more back in their home of long ago.

In August of that year the Carmelite International Congress was held in Rome. It was the seventh centenary celebration of the Brown Scapular.

Mother Teresa and Mother Mercedes were there for the opening meeting at the Teatro Adriano. Cardinal Piazza, himself a Carmelite, spoke but his talk was in Italian which was not too easy for them to follow. Later Father Killian Lynch, the prior general, spoke—and, to their delight, in English.

Next day Mother Mercedes joined the pilgrims to Vatican City, while Mother Teresa had an audience at Castel Gandolfo. The Assistant Carmelite general, Father Kenneth Leahy had offered to take two other Mothers General and Mother Teresa. One of the two others was a Spanish religious, the other was Mother Angeline Teresa of the Bronx Carmelites, who had been so generous with her car and driver when Mother Mary was making her long and difficult visitation.

Mother Teresa was surprised to find the papal palace completely hemmed in by small houses, some so close they all but touched it. She had expected to find long vistas everywhere but she had already noted that in Rome every bulding stands very close to the next, and it was the same here too.

The religious and their conductor, went past the Swiss guards, through several lovely rooms, and were told to wait. Suddenly there was a stir and the Holy Father walked into the room briskly and greeted them. He spoke Spanish to the Mother from Malaga and excellent English to the two religious from America.

Mother Teresa had been so excited by actually seeing the Holy Father himself right in front of her, by hearing his voice and receiving his blessing, that all the way back

*Mother Teresa, O. Carm.*
*elected second Superior General of the*
*Congregation*
*May 3, 1949*

to Rome she kept trying to fix in her mind just how he had looked so that she could tell the sisters at home. He seemed much younger than his years, she thought. The words "vigorous and frail" came, oddly enough, to her, as defining the tall figure in white.

The sisters called on Cardinal Fumasoni-Biondi and found him very interested in their work in Trinidad and especially interested in the growing number of their colored vocations there. He was delighted to learn that at the hospice for the aged the prioress was of Chinese and colored ancestry.

"She was born in Trinidad," explained Mother Teresa. "She is one of the first of our colored sisters. She is a very able and excellent administrator."

At their house in Tunapuna, the sisters told him, they had another Trinidadian prioress who was colored and a third in charge at Diego Martin who was of Portuguese ancestry. Now that educational facilities were open to all, there was no longer need of the extensive training of earlier years for the postulants. That was why they were now asking Rome for a two-year novitiate for them.

Cardinal Fumasoni-Biondi listened with pleasure to all this information, and said they were certainly fulfilling the Holy Father's special hope—the development of native vocations through the world. He knew the Pope would be happy to hear that they were fostering his hope so well.

For some time Mother Mary had been eager to open a foundation in South America and also to re-open the one in England. She died before this came about, but not long after her death both were established.

In 1950 a foundation was made in South America, at Georgetown in British Guiana. Mother Teresa went there with Mother Rita to open it. They stayed for more than a week with the Sisters of Mercy at Georgetown, as did the three sisters who came a little later as permanent members of the new mission.

The Sisters of Mercy were not only good hosts, but they gave their guests many gifts for the new hostel—a chalice, a sanctuary lamp, a new missal with "Corpus Christi Congregation" stamped on it, three beds with mattresses, and they loaned them prie-dieux until their stalls were ready. They gave them the use of their motor van and its driver. The newcomers said they had met with much generosity in their life but never more than this. Even after the sisters were settled in their new home, the Sisters of Mercy helped them by sewing for the new house and providing lunches for those who were working too hard to get settled to provide anything for themselves. And these sisters were busy teachers, whose days were already filled.

On February 11, the new St. Bernadette Hostel, named in honor of the saint of Lourdes, was blessed privately by the Vicar General. A week later the hostel was officially opened and blessed by Bishop Weld. Ten of his priests were present as guests, as well as a large number of lay people, many of whom brought gifts.

This mission was to be primarily a home for working girls, a home for them away from home, and at prices they could afford to pay. The cost of room and board had to be low for, as a rule, the girls made no more than three or four dollars a week. Ten girls had already moved in and many more were asking to come. The house was spacious, with cubicles for eighteen girls on the second floor and twelve more on the third. It also had a fine bicycle shed, a very necessary adjunct, for the whole island bicycled.

It had been due to the zeal and hard work of the Ladies of Charity of Georgetown that the hostel had been made possible. They were also assuming all costs of the hostel, but the sisters were to be in full charge there.

Back home again, Mother Teresa reported that, though perhaps British Guiana was not as beautiful as Trinidad, at least on the coast, for it was much more flat, the people were very warm hearted and friendly. Then, too, the sisters' house was close by the sea and a cool breeze blew nearly all the time.

Three years later the sisters opened a small mission at Springlands, some 120 miles from Georgetown. It took three hours to go those miles by ferry, bus and car. This was a little town whose one main street was lined with little wooden houses. There were few Catholics, and the church was very small. Many of the houses were on stilts, for often much of the land was under water; and British Guiana was six feet below sea level. Here at first the sisters taught chiefly pagan children. The population was chiefly Indian and there were few Catholics.

By 1951 plans were on foot for a return to England and the re-establishing of a house there. In that year, Mother Patricia went to England to take a fifteen-month refresher course in child care; this was considered necessary and useful for the type of work the sisters planned to do there.

She wrote home that at first Leicester had seemed to

her the city of long ago, but before she had been there long she found many changes. The lovely lanes down which the first members of the community used to walk evenings and Sundays were gone, lost to housing projects. But she also found that people felt much more kindly towards Catholics than they had in those early days.

The Bishop of Nottingham had asked the sisters to take charge of a home for small boys at Kirby Muxloe, a village on the outskirts of Leicester. And so in the spring of 1952, two sisters sailed from America to help make the foundation. Mother Mary's dream of an English house was being fulfilled. More than that, they would be a few miles from the spot where Queenie Ellerker and her mother and sister had come in 1908 to begin her work.

When Mother Teresa came there early in 1952, it was to her a going back to the past, to the days when as a young girl she had just entered the Church. But she was too busy with the present to have time to dwell long on the past. She and Mother Patricia and Sister Mary Joseph worked all day long making curtains—"miles of them"— and getting the house ready for occupancy.

The furniture which they bought for it was, in a way, a gift from Sister Josephine who had often expressed the wish that the small legacy she was leaving the community should be used towards a home for poor children. After her death, legal formalities took some time to clear the legacy and the money came just in time to be used for furniture for the small boys' rooms. It would have made Sister Josephine very happy indeed.

On March 21 Bishop Ellis came to bless the Home. Before he left he gave them the best gift he could possibly have given them: he placed the Blessed Sacrament in their chapel in the lovely little ciborium which he had himself given them. The next month Mother Teresa left for Trinidad by way of the United States, happy to know that the English house already had a postulant, Sister Elizabeth.

In Duluth, she told the story of their first small English boarder. Philip was five years old, and Sister Mary Joseph had taken him to town with her. She returned rather shattered in composure. "It has not been a dull afternoon," she reported. Philip had pretended to shoot everyone in the bus with his toy gun. He strutted down Leicester's main street holding Sister's mantle and shouting from its shelter, "Left, right," in martial tones. But next morning he had greeted her with his sweetest smile. "Are you pleased with me *this* morning, Sister?" he asked.

Soon more boys arrived at the new home; mostly they were children from broken homes who had known little love or attention in their short lives. One who looked like a brunette when he came turned out, after he had been given a thorough bath, to be the possessor of golden curls.

One small boy came to the home with a thoroughly frightened look on his face; from babyhood he had been moved about from one institution to another and was evidently apprehensive that this would be no better than the others had been. It did not take him long to change his expression after he found how comfortable was this, the first home he had ever known. Talking one day with a chance acquaintance in the village about the sisters at Kirby Muxloe, he said, with a lingering surprise still on his face, "They really *want* me, you know."

The congregation wished to open a novitiate in England but, since a home for noisy boys was hardly the best place, they began searching for another house to meet that purpose.

Two years later they found it, at Shorne, an ancient town and once a very Catholic one. Here, in addition to the house which they bought, was a wonderful little chapel which was the property of the owners of the house, but given some years before to the diocese. St. Katherine's Chapel, which had been its name since the thirteenth century, was a little flint stone church which had been suppressed under Henry VIII, sold to laymen by Elizabeth, and later made into a malthouse and at another time into a stable. Bought in the nineteenth century by a Jewish convert who had been instructed in the Faith by Cardinal Manning, Mr. Arnold had had the little building restored to its original form and use.

On August 22, 1954, the Corpus Christi Sisters chanted vespers for the first time in St. Katherine's Chapel while all about them was evidence of the age of Faith in England, as shown in the ancient timbers and walls. Their own house was a very old one too, with great beams and teak paneling. Beyond the rose bushes in the spacious yard one could see the shimmer of the Thames.

The house was officially opened by Bishop Cowdroy in September. He told the sisters that he was happy they had taken the house. "Now I shall not have to worry about the chapel either," he said. "And since your sisters bear the name of Corpus Christi I know I shall not have to worry about one other thing: you will take good care of the Blessed Sacrament."

Within the year the house at Shorne, now the English novitiate, looked very different than it had the day the sisters came there. The unkept hedges and lawns were clipped and cut, and there were flowers everywhere. Even at Christmas small flowers bloomed at their door step. They had visitors too, for Aylesford sent its first group of pilgrims to see Shorne and St. Katherine's, a landmark of the Faith, and the little medieval chapel where no Mass had been said for hundreds of years and where now there was a daily Mass. As long ago, the little house of God again held on its altar the Blessed Sacrament. The sisters had been delighted to learn that the Guild which had been in charge of the chapel in the middle ages had been named the Corpus Christi Guild.

By spring of 1956 Shorne had a chaplain, a house for him, and the first Shorne-trained novice had made her temporary vows.

They were very proud of their chaplain. Father Bernard Kelly was not young nor very strong, but he was an historian of note, and he had written many books, as well as the supplement to Butler's *Lives of the Saints*. His special love was the history of the Stuarts and their life in exile. He brought to his new home a fine library of two thousand volumes. The sisters were proud of this too, but when they saw the boxes being unpacked, they groaned. "Where shall we put them?" they wondered.

In 1954 the sisters at Middletown celebrated the silver anniversary of their arrival there. To many it seemed impossible that so many years had passed since they first came there, since Miss Murphy's furniture, including the piano and the apples, had come to a small group just getting ready to function.

Father Patrick Russell, the Carmelite provincial, gave

the discourse at the High Mass which celebrated the occasion, and he chose as his text one from Deuteronomy which was very appropriate: "The Lord thy God carried thee all the way you have come until you came to this house."

In the year following, a new Carmel was opened in the United States, this one at Newport, Rhode Island. It was a fine house and in a beautiful location on Narragansett Bay.

For a long time there had been discussion of a novitiate in the eastern part of the country, and the sisters had looked at various properties, none of which seemed suitable. One day a letter came from the Religious of the Cenacle, stating that their own convent in Newport was for sale. They were anxious to leave their home of fifty years in the hands of a religious congregation and especially one which would carry on their own work of retreats. The religious were leaving there, they explained, only because other foundations were greatly in need of sisters.

Their description of the property, sent with the letter, sounded almost too good to be true; but the letter was sent on to Mother Teresa, who suggested that two sisters go to look it over. They found that the description had not been exaggerated.

Four religious still remained at the convent, and they would remain until the new owners took over. They showed them the house and grounds and the large chapel, beautifully paneled in dark wood with white tiled floors, the spacious choir, and room for a hundred people in the body of the building; the marble altar and fine stained glass windows.

The decision was made to acquire the property and a group went to take possession soon afterwards. Moving vans preceded the sisters in their station wagon. In the vans were, among the other furniture, the first choir stalls ever used in Middletown and which had been designed by Mother Mary of the Blessed Sacrament.

In the station wagon with the sisters was a statue of Our Lady of Mount Carmel. It had been at Middletown, on a table placed just outside the chapel, waiting to be taken to any house she might select for the new foundation.

The sisters of the Cenacle were still there, ready to leave as soon as the new owners arrived. They were leaving some of their furniture behind, they told the grateful newcomers. Later in the day the departing religious said goodbye to their old home. The Corpus Christi Sisters went to the chapel to recite with joyous hearts the Vespers of the Annunciation in the choir of their new Carmel.

In 1957 the Superior General went on a visitation of her houses. By that time there were several new ones to greet her. One was at Grenada, a hundred miles from Port of Spain, and founded by her in person the year before.

Grenada, a beautiful island of volcanic origin, was hilly and irregular. Both school and Carmel were on the beach itself, one famed for its beauty. At the school the sisters taught some 250 children of primary standards. As for their own convent, it was so close to the ocean that they called it Carmel-by-the-sea and boasted that one could go fishing from their verandah.

Another foundation recently opened was that at St. Lucia, another beautiful island, and some hundred and fifty miles from Trinidad. Here the sisters staffed a home for the aged. At Castries, the capital of the island, many people were destitute. A home had been set up for old men but the old women were lodged in very poor quarters. The parish priest had been for some time collecting funds to build a home to house them all. Then an old Santa Lucian settled the priest's problem by giving a large sum "for the benefit of the poor." Father Florissac, long resident in the United States, had sent his old home the wonderful gift of nine thousand dollars, and so the Marian Home was erected and furnished, and the Corpus Christi Sisters were invited to staff it.

To this house flocked the old people—the blind, the weak, the lame, several of them over ninety years old. Not only did the new home help the tired old bodies; it helped the souls, and some who had been away from the sacraments for forty years and more, now returned to their duties.

The Superior General found at the new Home two blind boys who were to remain for a time since there was no other place for them. One owned a mouth organ and, when they learned the other could play it too, the sisters procured one for him. Then there was much gay playing which helped make life pleasanter for their guests.

"They seem able to play anything," Mother Teresa wrote home in admiration of their talents. "The old ladies dance in the front gallery, the old men on the porch. And there is always a crowd in the yard listening and some of them are dancing too."

At the English house the membership had increased. In the United States a new Carmel had been set up, as well as a kindergarten and day nursery, in Philadelphia. The houses in the northwest were humming with activity and in Newport the novitiate was flourishing, as was the work in Middletown.

Everywhere was a demand for more members than they could provide. Everywhere the congregation had to turn down the offer of new foundations because they had not enough members to staff them all. But they accepted what they could, even though the members were still few. They still showed the willingness which Father McNabb had admired in them in the first years of their work—a willingness to spread themselves recklessly, as he had put it.

At that time they had had scarcely any members, but already they had gone to Trinidad and to the United States. Now, in 1957, they were still spreading recklessly. In that year the Superior General's visitation included two Carmels in England, two in South America, six in the British West Indies, and seven in the United States. They had four novitiates—at Shorne, at Port of Spain, at Kearney and at Newport.

Early in 1958 wonderful news came to the Corpus Christi Carmelites. A cable came from Rome, dated February 18, sent to Trinidad by Father Killian Lynch, prior general of the Carmelite Order. The congregation of Corpus Christi Carmelites had received their Final Approval.

This would give them pontifical status and also a great sense of future security. Father Lynch had worked hard to secure it for them and their own Archbishop Finbar Ryan, had been of great help.

"You and the Congregation have my heartiest congratulations on the attainment of the goal on which we fixed our eyes and hearts eighteen years ago," he wrote to the Superior General. "Please God and Our Lady of Mount Carmel, the new pontifical status of the Congregation will ensure its increasing success in the formation, internally, of Saints; externally, of social work according to the mind of Our Lord."

When word reached the other Carmels of the congregation, there was equally great thankfulness and joy. There was a deep happiness at this wonderful fulfillment of their prayers.

Since the day the few came together in the house at Leicester, the record of the group of Dominican tertiaries who became Corpus Christi Carmelites has been one of continual faithfulness. This had been reflected in the number of prelates who have asked them to work in their dioceses.

The beginnings were very small and informal—a handful of converts who grew into the religious life and who stayed together. What they lacked in numbers they made up for in assiduity, in intelligence, in an ability to work together for good.

This they have done and are still doing. And perhaps one very important reason is that the valiant woman who headed them for so many years, even when she was immobilized by a painful disease, is still with them all. On earth she inspired them in their work. In Heaven she is praying for them.

*Most Reverend Kilian E. Lynch, O. Carm.*
*Prior General*